Art and Order

ART AND ORDER

A Study of E. M. Forster

By ALAN WILDE

NEW YORK UNIVERSITY PRESS   1964

For permission to quote from the works of E. M. Forster thanks are due to Mr. Forster and to the following publishers: *Howards End, The Longest Journey, A Room with a View,* and *Where Angels Fear to Tread* (Alfred A. Knopf, Inc. and Edward Arnold Ltd.); *Abinger Harvest, Aspects of the Novel, Goldsworthy Lowes Dickinson,* and *A Passage to India* (Harcourt, Brace & World, Inc. and Edward Arnold Ltd.); *The Hill of Devi, The Eternal Moment and Other Stories* (including "The Machine Stops," "The Point of It," "Mr. Andrews," "Co-ordination," "The Story of the Siren," and "The Eternal Moment"), *Marianne Thornton,* and *Two Cheers for Democracy* (Harcourt, Brace & World, Inc.); *The Collected Tales of E. M. Forster* (Alfred A. Knopf, Inc.); *England's Pleasant Land* (The Hogarth Press). Thanks are also due to *Modern Fiction Studies* and the Purdue Research Foundation for permission to reprint the chapter on *Where Angels Fear to Tread,* which appeared originally in *Modern Fiction Studies,* VII (Autumn, 1961).

For Dora and for Betty and Rose

ACKNOWLEDGMENTS

I wish to thank Professor Douglas Bush and Professor Reuben A. Brower for the patience and care with which they read an earlier version of this book, Williams College for aid from its 1900 Fund, and Mr. Forster for his generosity in answering questions about his work and in allowing me to discuss it with him. I am particularly indebted to Professor Jack Undank, who has read a number of versions of this book with sympathy and understanding. His perceptive criticisms have provided me with many valuable insights, of which I have made use in the pages that follow.

CONTENTS

Art and Order

1 · Art and Life: Biographical and Introductory

THE OPENING LINE of *Howards End*—"One may as well begin with Helen's letter to her sister"—is a perfect example of what one of Christopher Isherwood's characters refers to as Forster's tea-tabling. The remark is so casual and understated, the tone so relaxed and personal; here we are, almost before we know it, in the complicated world of the Schlegels and the Wilcoxes. Or the beginning of "Anonymity: An Enquiry," a well-known essay by Forster: "Do you like to know who a book's by?" (*TC*, p. 77).[1] Do we? How flattering it is to have our opinion asked . . . and here we are again, this time in Forster's own world, involved in the process of discovery, sharing the sense of intimacy it is Forster's particular gift to create. This is the voice with which Forster has spoken out over several decades for the importance of the individual and his personal relations, for the value of tolerance, sympathy, and good temper, for the desirability of variety and pleasure in an increasingly gloomy and uniform world; the voice also with which he has attacked, wherever he found them, the abuses of authority and the perils of what he has called, in describing the English, "the undeveloped heart." And we are tempted, in an age of propaganda and advertise-

1 All references to Forster's works will be given in parentheses immediately following the material quoted. A note on the editions used precedes the Bibliography. The following abbreviations appear in the book: AH = *Abinger Harvest*; AN = *Aspects of the Novel*; CT = *The Collected Tales*; EPL = *England's Pleasant Land*; GLD = *Goldworthy Lowes Dickinson*; MT = *Marianne Thornton*; PI = *A Passage to India*; TC = *Two Cheers for Democracy*; WAFTT = *Where Angels Fear to Tread*.

1

ment, to listen to someone who refuses to speak in loud and commanding tones, who is hesitant, cautious, acutely aware, even self-conscious, who is—like ourselves.

It was this aspect of Forster which appealed so strongly to the young men of the 1930's, and particularly to the members of the so-called Auden group, who took him as their symbol of liberal, skeptical humanism and found in him an ally against what they called "the old gang"—the forces of conservatism and reaction at home—and against the growing threat of fascism abroad. "Here, though the bombs are real and dangerous," W. H. Auden writes in a sonnet addressed to Forster, ". . . You promise still the inner life shall pay." And the narrator of Isherwood's latest novel records in his diary for 1938 (by way of attacking Chamberlain) this impression of Forster:

Well, my "England" is E.M.; the antiheroic hero. . . . While the others tell their followers to be ready to die, he advises us to live as if we were immortal. And he really does this himself, although he is as anxious and afraid as any of us, and never for an instant pretends not to be. He and his books and what they stand for are all that is truly worth saving from Hitler.[2]

Isherwood's remarks make clear that Forster, in the years before the war, was already becoming the touchstone of a particular set of values and attitudes. In the years since, largely because of his essays and his broadcasts, he has reached a wider public than his novels had ever brought him and has become, ironically, something of an institution. Ironically, because Forster is the most individualistic of writers and because, as William Plomer pointed out on the occasion of his eightieth birthday, he "has taken care not to groom himself for the role of a Grand Old Man, by self-advertisement or any other means."[3] But if

2 The references to Auden and Isherwood are as follows: the remarks about tea-tabling appear in *Lions and Shadows* (London: The Hogarth Press, 1938), pp. 173–75; the phrase "the old gang" is from Auden's poem "1929," which can be found in *The Collected Poetry* (New York: Random House, 1945), p. 67; the sonnet is the prefatory poem to Auden's and Isherwood's *Journey to a War* (London: Faber and Faber, 1939); the last quotation is from *Down There on a Visit* (New York: Simon and Schuster, 1962), p. 162. A number of interesting comparisons between Forster and Isherwood are made by K. W. Grandsen in his *E. M. Forster* (New York: Grove Press, 1962).

3 William Plomer, "Foreword," *The London Magazine*, VI (January, 1959), 9.

Forster has refused to become a literary mandarin, he is at least in part responsible for becoming what Lionel Trilling calls a literary figure, one of those who "preside, as it were, over certain ideas and attitudes." Forster he sees as someone who "acts out in public the role of the private man, becoming for us the very spirit of the private life." [4] In other words, we were mistaken in imagining that we had penetrated to the inner sanctum; we accepted the illusion of intimacy for the reality and felt we had come to know Forster himself. In fact, we know only so much about Forster as he has been willing to tell us, and that, after all, is not much.

Max Beerbohm, in a brilliant parody of literary and biographical criticism, describes his hero's life as one "happily not void of those sensational details which are what we all really care about." If such details are part of Forster's life, they have not been revealed. His intimate self, unlike Gide's, Mauriac's or J. C. Powys' in their lifetimes, strains toward privacy and even secrecy: he has written no autobiography, has censored the few letters which give promise of some deeper revelation,[5] and has published only fragments of his diaries and journals.[6] Whenever he does assess his life publically, it is generally laid out in a formative, developmental perspective, describing principally the etiology of certain values and beliefs. This is obviously the approach he favors. He tells us of the forces that helped mold his thought, of a series of monumental encounters with places and individuals, but the feel of living with those thoughts and that formation is absent.

The only sustained account of himself Forster has published—and that, recently, in 1956—is shyly hidden behind a tribute to his great-aunt, Marianne Thornton. The last section of the biography begins with Forster's birth on January 1, 1879, and ends with her death shortly before his ninth birthday. But even here personal development is subsumed to intellectual. He makes little, for example, of the fact that his childhood was passed mainly among women, in the absence of his father, who

4 Lionel Trilling, "George Orwell and the Politics of Truth," *The Opposing Self* (London: Secker & Warburg, 1955), pp. 155–56.
5 See A. W. Lawrence (ed.), *Letters to T. E. Lawrence* (London: Jonathan Cape, 1962), pp. 58–75.
6 See "The Last of Abinger," *TC*, pp. 358–63; and "Indian Entries," *Encounter*, XVIII (January, 1962), 20–27.

had died before his son was two, or that "The Important One,"
as he was called, succeeded his father in his great-aunt's affections. A supposedly delicate, an undoubtedly clever, spoiled, and
overprotected child, Forster grew up in Hertfordshire with his
mother, in the house which was to serve as a model for Mrs.
Wilcox's home in *Howards End*. Characteristically, it is the
house that takes Forster's attention away from the child:

> From the time I entered the house at the age of four . . . I took
> it to my heart and hoped . . . that I should live and die there.
> We were out of it in ten years. The impressions received there re-
> mained and still glow—not always distinguishably, always inex-
> tinguishably—and have given me a slant upon society and history.
> It is a middle-class slant, atavistic, derived from the Thorntons. (p.
> 301)

Forster is quick to find and project here, as in his fiction,
symbols which act as polarities for belief. He grew up between
the signs of Battersea Rise, the house of his ancestors, the
Thorntons, stable, traditional, producing "the family life that
does not die with death" (p. 41), and the Wichelos, his mother's
relatives, who "had no enthusiasm for work . . . were devoid of
public spirit, and . . . were averse to piety and quick to detect
the falsity sometimes accompanying it" (pp. 278–79). From
the one he acquired a sense of place and continuity, to counter,
however imperfectly, the change, urbanization, and fragmenta-
tion of modern life; from the other, an individualistic rebellious-
ness against Thornton stolidity: their inflexible religious beliefs,
their philistine attitude toward art, and their rigid, moral distinctions.[7] In any case, whatever else Forster may have inherited
from his family, he received more concretely, on Marianne
Thornton's death, £8000, which enabled him to attend Cambridge, to travel, and to write. "Her love," his book ends, "in
a most tangible sense, followed me beyond the grave" (p. 325).

In the succeeding years, which can be pieced together in
the special light he himself provides, Forster attended Ton-

---

7 On the Clapham Sect, in which Forster's great-grandfather, Henry
Thornton, figured prominently, see Noel Annan, "The Intellectual Aris-
tocracy," in *Studies in Social History: A Tribute to G. M. Trevelyan*, ed.
by J. H. Plumb (London: Longmans, Green, 1955), pp. 241–87; and
Annan's *Leslie Stephen: His Thought and Character in Relation to his
Time* (Cambridge, Mass.: Harvard University Press, 1952), pp. 110–26.

bridge School and then King's College, Cambridge. His experiences at both, we know, furnished the basis for Rickie Elliot's feelings about Sawston School and the university in *The Longest Journey*. More than that, they provided him with symbols of two different ways of life, which are contrasted throughout his works: Tonbridge apparently taught him the essential disorder of human existence and gave him his hatred of injustice, cruelty, and stupidity; Cambridge, the counterideal—the possibility of inclusion, unity, order. In his biography of Goldsworthy Lowes Dickinson, Forster writes with fellow feeling of the impact of King's College on his friend:

As Cambridge filled up with friends it acquired a magic quality. Body and spirit, reason and emotion, work and play, architecture and scenery, laughter and seriousness, life and art—these pairs which are elsewhere contrasted were there fused into one. People and books reinforced one another, intelligence joined hands with affection, speculation became a passion, and discussion was made profound by love. (p. 35)

According to F. R. Leavis, there is something sentimental and uncritical about Forster's Cambridge.[8] Many others, however, from Samuel Butler to G. E. Moore and Bertrand Russell, have indicated that they felt as Forster did.[9] What is certain is that the period between 1897 and 1901 constituted for Forster "the magic years," as Rickie Elliot calls them (p. 192), the time particularly of good-fellowship and friendship. Although Forster, typically, reveals nothing about his contemporaries in his study of Dickinson, his remarks about his tutors and their generation help to define the qualities which attracted him in others. Roughly speaking, what he liked in Nathaniel Wedd and Oscar Browning, his classics and history tutors, was less their intellectual superiority than their moral characters. Not that either was in a conventional sense a good man—Browning he

8 F. R. Leavis, "Meet Mr. Forster," *Scrutiny*, XII (Autumn, 1944), 308.

9 See Samuel Butler *The Way of All Flesh* (London: Jonathan Cape, 1925), pp. 195–96; G. E. Moore "An Autobiography," *The Philosophy of G. E. Moore*, ed. by P. A. Schilpp (Evanston and Chicago: Northwestern University, 1942), pp. 12–13; and Bertrand Russell "My Mental Development," *The Philosophy of Bertrand Russell*, ed. by P. A. Schilpp (New York: Tudor Publishing Company, 1951), pp. 8–9.

compares to Silenus, Wedd to Mephistopheles—but then that
is not a type Forster has ever admired. Eccentric and individual,
both men were active, warm, outgoing; both liked people; and
both enjoyed teaching young men, or, rather, teaching young
men to know themselves. "It is to him," Forster writes of Wedd,
". . . that I owe such awakening as has befallen me. It is
through him that I can best imagine the honesty and fervour of
fifty years back" (p. 73). Dickinson himself Forster became
friendly with only later on. A quieter man than the other two,
he shared with them an interest in human beings and an active
concern with things outside himself. "Indeed, to a Goth like myself," Forster comments, "he seems much more Socratic than
Socrates" (p. 46), and it is at least possible that, along with
Wedd and Browning, Dickinson served as the model for the
Socratic characters, like Mr. Failing in *The Longest Journey* or
Mr. Emerson in *A Room with a View*, who appear in almost
all of the novels and whose wisdom is always on the side of
participation in life.

The most famous of Forster's friends were members of the
Bloomsbury Group, which came into active being in the early
years of the century. The nucleus of the group consisted of
Virginia Woolf, Clive and Vanessa Bell, Duncan Grant, Roger
Fry, Lytton Strachey, and John Maynard Keynes: writers, artists,
and thinkers sharing common ideas and ideals and to a large
degree a common background, since most of them derived from
the families which Noel Annan has called the "Intellectual
Aristocracy" of the nineteenth century.[10] Much has been written
to show Forster's connection with them.[11] In particular, J. K.
Johnstone, in his study of Woolf, Strachey, and Forster, has
demonstrated the influence on all three of the artistic theories
of Fry and Bell and of the philosophy of G. E. Moore, with its
emphasis on states of mind connected with aesthetic contem-
plation and personal relations. Certainly, in his concern for the

10 See footnote 7, above.
11 See J. K. Johnstone, *The Bloomsbury Group: A Study of E. M.
Forster, Lytton Strachey, Virginia Woolf, and Their Circle* (New York:
Noonday, 1954). Frederick C. Crews' *E. M. Forster: The Perils of Humanism* (Princeton, N. J.: Princeton University Press, 1962), Chapters
II–IV, deals more broadly with the intellectual background of Forster's
thought.

inner life, in his agnosticism and humanism, and in his belief in art for its own sake, Forster has affinities with the others. But it is still more interesting to note that, as usual, Forster eludes categories: as writer and thinker his beliefs are less radical, his techniques less experimental; as a friend, he seems to have remained, on the testimony of those who composed it, on the fringes of the circle. Typical of the attitude of most of Bloomsbury's original members is Keynes's description of Forster as "the elusive colt of a dark horse." [12] a phrase which may stand more generally as an index to Forster's fundamental sense of privacy.

In part, Forster's relation—or lack of relation—to Bloomsbury can be explained by the fact that he was so often in these years out of London, where the group had its center. Between 1901 and 1921 the facts of Forster's life are a record of his travels. Marianne Thornton's legacy took him first to Italy and Greece, which, as a number of articles in *Abinger Harvest*, most of the early short stories, and the two "Italian" novels show, provided a stimulus to, and a form for, his primitivism. Or perhaps, in the case of Greece, one should say that his travels made vivid what he had already learned as a student of classics at Cambridge. Dickinson's *The Greek View of Life* (1896) is a lucid summary of the Hellenism that was popular at the time, and both the quality and the force of its enthusiasm for Greece carry over into Forster's books. When Helen Schlegel tells her sister in *Howards End*, "You're a heroine. . . . You mean to keep proportion, and that's heroic, it's Greek" (p. 205), she is updating the Dickinsonian ideal of harmony and balance, of a unity of the inner and the outer, of body and soul, of the aesthetic and the ethical.

Italy, more directly, offered Forster a sense of liberation, a contrast to English repressive conventionality, and an answer on a larger scale than Cambridge's to the dreary world of Sawston. In his early work especially, Italy is Forster's symbol of natural order, a country full of light and air where men act spontaneously and where the artificial barriers that separate them almost magically fall away; there communication takes place in a

12 John Maynard Keynes, *Two Memoirs* (New York: Augustus M. Kelley, 1949), p. 81.

medium of complete transparency. Like Greece, Italy suggests
an apparently effortless harmony which is in fact the result of
countless ages of accumulated tradition and of living close to
the earth. The Pans and Demeters who crowd Forster's fiction
at this time are invariably associated with the land, with vitality
and fullness of living. The characters they accompany or to
whom they reveal themselves are Forster's heroes, the unself-
conscious and frequently anti-intellectual men and women who
are generally so different from his protagonists and from himself.

In 1905, Forster was in Germany as tutor to the children
of the Countess von Arnim.[13] His impressions of the months
he spent there later found their way into *Howards End*, where
Germany figures both as a contrast and as a warning to England.
The contrast is suggested by the fact that Mr. Schlegel, the
German-born father of Forster's heroines, has left his country
in protest against its abandonment of the idealistic tradition he
himself represents. The sword he had used in the Franco-Prus-
sian War, now sheathed and hanging over the mantle, is a
symbol throughout the book of the change from idealism to
materialism and of the unsuccessful attempt to beat the sword
back into a ploughshare. His daughters, however, are aware that
England is fast following, in some respects leading, Germany
in the race towards bigness, philistinism, and stupidity, and it
is one of Forster's main designs to show that England is threatened even more from within than from without. Forster stands
for the small, the personal, the unorganized and unmechanized,
and it is the passing of these that he fears even more than the
coming of war, which the book predicts.

When the war did come four years later, Forster volun-
teered for the Red Cross and spent the years from 1915 to 1918
in Alexandria. In *A Passage to India*, Forster referred to the
Mediterranean as "the human norm" (p. 293), and his return to
it inspired two of his most humanistic works, *Alexandria, A
History and a Guide* and *Pharos and Pharillon*. They are not,
unfortunately, among his best, and their chief interest is in the
way they illustrate his abiding distrust of Christianity. To Forster, Christianity, at least when it is in a position of power,

13 See Forster's "Recollections of Nassenheide," *The Listener*, LXI
(January 1, 1959), 12–14.

suggests aggressiveness, intolerance, obscurantism, and asceticism, to which he opposes the pagan elements in Alexandrian culture. The object of Forster's attack is ostensibly the church of the first five centuries after Christ, but the reader is meant to make contemporary inferences and connections, to recognize in Christianity another form of self-assured and false pretension to order and truth.

The war and even more his two trips to India in 1912–13 and 1921 helped make Forster still more doubtful about the possibility of order and truth in his world. Both upset still further the steadiness of his outlook, the one by its disruption of traditional English institutions, the other by intensifying the relativism implicit in all his fiction. One might not think so to read *The Hill of Devi*, a collection of Forster's puzzled and critical letters retailing news of India to the family back home, but in *A Passage to India* he symbolically transmutes his experience into a profound pessimism. In the face of the confusion and muddle of the East, even the comparative certainties of Italy and Greece give way. It was, then, after 1924 that Forster ceased publishing novels, according to his own account because "the social aspect of the world changed so much." Still he continued to write, essays principally, but also biography and criticism: "I wanted to write, but did not want to write novels . . . and though I can think about the new world I cannot put it into fiction." [14] The thirties and forties are Forster's great period in the essay. He continued to travel, notably to South Africa, to the United States in 1946, to Greece and Italy again in the fifties. Lecturing, making radio broadcasts for the B.B.C., addressing P.E.N. conferences, he has been increasingly accepted, despite his failure to produce any more fiction, as England's greatest living novelist as well as its symbol of the "anti-heroic hero." In 1946, Forster left his home in Abinger, Surrey, to become an honorary fellow of his old college, where he continues to live—a very welcome visitor, to judge by the tributes he received on his eightieth birthday when Noel Annan, provost

---

14 David Jones, "E. M. Forster on his Life and his Books," *The Listener*, LXI (January 1, 1959), 11. An interesting study of Forster that leads up to the reasons for his having ceased writing novels is C. B. Cox's in his *The Free Spirit* (London: Oxford, 1963), Chapter IV.

of King's, compared him, as once he had his friend Dickinson, to Socrates.[15]

Personally, Forster is a man of great charm. Soft and mild in his manner, he makes conversation easy and pleasant, provided, at any rate, that the conversation is not about himself. In the latter case, he is apt to change the subject and move unobtrusively onto more neutral and less personal ground. There is no doubt of Forster's interest in other people or of his ability to make them believe that their opinions are important to him. But one is likely to feel that the counterpart of his concern for others is a distinct reticence about himself. It would seem to be neither an accident nor the fault of those to whom he was speaking that Forster has so often said the same things in his interviews: others besides this writer have felt the presence of barriers beyond which it is impossible to go. No one has summed up this quality in Forster better than Frank Swinnerton: "He is one of the very few men by whom I am consciously affected; by which I mean that something in him moves me to a slightly exaggerated boisterousness of behaviour. I should not mention this if I had not found that he causes others also to feel coltish. But the fault is not in him; one has the sense of perfect integrity, calm, sympathy; however a little remoteness too." [16]

There would seem to be a correlation between the remoteness Swinnerton finds and the sparseness of the available, more intimate biographical material. In any case, there is considerable difficulty in trying to approach Forster simply from the outside and a danger that one will confuse the "literary figure" with the man himself. In fact, the best way to get at Forster is through his works, particularly the fiction, through what Ortega y Gasset called "biografía desde dentro"—the evolving themes, preoccupations, and conflicts that the works, implicitly or explicitly, express. In this "biography" of the inner life, the sense of mastery and "living as though one were immortal" gives way to an interior, dialectical struggle. For there is everywhere in Forster's novels a sense of opposition and twoness; dealing with a series

15 See Mollie Panter-Downes, "Kingsman," New Yorker, XXXV (September 19, 1959), 51.

16 Frank Swinnerton, The Georgian Scene: A Literary Panorama (New York: Farrar & Rinehart, 1934), p. 390.

of related problems in which two forces struggle with one another, each novel reaches, tentatively and hesitantly, a solution which the next, beginning the search over again, disrupts. There are no decisive battles in Forster's world, only skirmishes and the sense that it is all to do once more. Repeatedly, the symbols of the "natural" life of activity and involvement—Italy, Greece, the English countryside, to mention only the most outstanding —face London, Sawston, Christianity, and whatever else suggests the life of passivity, rigidity, and nonparticipation. Briefly, the struggle, in the early novels particularly, is between what will be called in the following pages "the aesthetic view of life"— that is to say, the habit of responding to life as if it had the permanence and fixity, the shape and coherence of a work of art [17] and, as Mr. Emerson puts it in *A Room with a View*, standing in the sun and living for all one is worth.

But the abstract formulation of Forster's dominant theme and even the solution of the conflict it presents tell only part of the story; his profoundest attitudes reveal themselves only in his treatment of that theme. This, oddly enough, suggests a kind of counterrevolution of sympathies. It is clear, for example, to the most casual reader that Mr. Emerson and his sort are meant to suggest the ideal. It is equally clear that they are the least interesting and the least adequately developed of his characters, that they remain not only ideal but idealized figures who persuade us not of their own reality, but of their importance to the author. As such, they frequently threaten to wreck the books of which they are part: they have the resonance not of what Forster would call round characters, but of fantasy figures, like those who in the short stories escape from the un-

[17] Art itself for Forster is a selection from the multiplicity and confusion of life and an arrangement of the chosen details into something unique. The process whereby art is produced and the state of mind it entails represent something valuable, but—and this is the crucial point— their value lies in the fact that they are a *means* towards the creation of works of art, which are ultimately independent of their creators. When, however, the aesthetic view of life becomes an end in itself, when the detachment it requires serves to keep men from a necessary participation in the fullness and diversity of living, it turns into something pernicious, sterile, and self-defeating. Its practitioners are those who, for whatever reasons, seek overmuch for an unchanging order in life, and its end product is a frame of mind that is both rigid and narrow.

satisfactoriness of daily life into some more significant realm of being. The contest, seen at this artistic level, between the heroes and the failures (who are generally the protagonists of the fiction) is entirely unequal, and the failures win not because Forster is trying to say so, but because the heroes are off fighting on another plain. Forster's inability to join their two worlds is acknowledged in the stories; in the novels, where the Ginos and Stephens presumably triumph in this world, a pretense of connection is made. But for all the warmth and activity they are meant to symbolize, they are in fact abstract and chill and, not entirely against Forster's deeper will, the reader's sympathies are generally with those whose attitudes he ought to condemn: the inveterate but understandable spectators of life.

One can accept Forster's primitivist heroes as pointers toward the good life, as objects of a faith which cannot be fully conceived or articulated, but it is his problem children who are the real centers of his repeated attention and insight: they concern him more fundamentally and more personally than the others attract him, and for that very reason they come off far worse. He treats them not only more thoroughly, but cruelly, and—it is interesting to note—with the very same cruelty of which only those spectators of life, like Philip Herriton and Cecil Vyse, are capable. There is, in fact, a great deal of the spectator in Forster himself, as his self-identification with Cecil, Philip, and Rickie Elliot would suggest.[18] One senses in him the same theoretical attraction to the life of activity, the same temperamental bias toward detachment. All impulses in Forster's books generate, by what seems almost a law of cause and effect, their opposites: so hope breeds despair, and assurance, doubt, and the movement toward the personal entails retreat into the private.

This movement has far-reaching artistic implications. Forster's famous irony, which is not simply an isolated technique but a state of mind, is actually a brilliant extension of, or foil to, the intimate voice that the Auden group admired. And just

18 P. N. Furbank and F. J. H. Haskell, "E. M. Forster," *Writers at Work,* ed. by Malcolm Cowley (New York: Viking Press, 1958), pp. 32–33.

as Forster maintains an ambiguous love-hate attitude toward his protagonists, so his narrators draw the reader into their confidence only to destroy their own and the reader's involvement with these same characters. The result is that we are constantly jostled out of our comfortable sympathies and asked to stand back and view the scene with the narrator's complicitous detachment. Forster expands and shrinks the aesthetic distance in a tantalizing movement of involvement and disengagement, of love and scorn. It becomes apparent to a close reader of all the novels that controlling this artistic device is a mind extraordinarily aware, even afraid, of the mysteries of self-forgetfulness. A moment's involvement is met by a cold awakening. The reader enjoys the wit and variety, but from the center of Forster's creations, his protagonists send out signals that they care to be loved and pitied, that they want to be part of life; still, though they often make the effort, they cannot or dare not. And on the outer edges of their lives, the narrator, prodded on by Forster's deepest impulse, gives them a fullness of existence, only suddenly to withdraw from artistic involvement, as they do from life, and to mock them—even, with what Auden has called the negative inversion of the will, to maim or destroy them completely.

Destructiveness is the mode of the early books particularly, but this is not to say that their intention is negative. Like Gide's they are concerned with clearing away old wood, and they are based on the unstated and hopeful assumption that the elimination or at least the acknowledgment of what is wrong will ensure the establishment of the good. Forster himself obviously came to feel that his assumption was a facile one, and his dissatisfaction with the solutions he had so far achieved and the direction he had so far followed is apparent in the fact that his later works, though they continue to take notice of the problem of aesthetic detachment, focus differently. In them there is apparent what the assault against the aesthetic view of life had partially concealed from the reader and from Forster himself— the feeling, which is apparent to some degree in all the fiction, that life is fundamentally disordered, that at its very foundations the universe is chaotic. It is a feeling that explains why the search for order motivates and dominates Forster's thought and why, after the oblique treatment of the early works, it becomes the leading theme of the later fiction.

It is no longer, then, after A Room with a View, simply a question of ridding the world of false orders, but of somehow finding a new and binding coherence, and Forster's search is both more positive and intense and, at the same time, increasingly less confident. Howards End, with its epigraph "Only connect," is his boldest and most ambitious step in that direction. The novel has an upward design; it ends ostensibly on a note of triumph: the world is connected, but it is badly soldered. Forster's symbols again betray that typical fall from the grace of reality that is his special mark of inner and artistic failure. It is only in A Passage to India, Forster's greatest novel, but his last, that he comes finally to acknowledge fully and consciously the abyss that underlies man's fragile, changing, and disordered world. And if the pursuit of order leads the novelist, paradoxically, to strike and explore a level of consciousness that threatens despair and moral paralysis, the same pursuit, now even more desperate for its discoveries, helps steer him away from the novel toward the essay, away from the permanent chaos toward the consciously controlled illumination of nonfiction.

This is to say that Forster's nonfiction operates only on a certain level, that it accepts what has been called "the philosophy of 'As if' " [19]: "One must behave as if one is immortal, and as if civilization is eternal," he writes in the essay to which Isherwood has referred. "Both statements are false . . . both of them must be assumed to be true if we are to go on eating and working and travelling, and keep open a few breathing holes for the human spirit" (AH, p. 85). In other words, man must not deny, but he must ignore, the horror of the world, if he is to make anything of it. Throughout Forster's nonfiction runs the generally unstated awareness of death, change, and separation, but his essays are constructive in intent: they aim to show how one ought to live despite these facts. This they do, finally, by returning to the problem of art, to its positive uses rather than, as in the early fiction, its abuses. After his long fight against

19 See Hans Vaihinger, The Philosophy of "As if," trans. C. K. Ogden (New York: Harcourt, Brace & Co., 1924).

the aesthetic view of life and his even longer struggle to discover order, he finds in the harmony of art a symbol of the best
man has done and may do in the face of the increasing disinte-
gration of his world. If Forster's artistic achievement culminates
in *A Passage to India*, it is in the essays which follow that the
dialectic of his thought achieves its equilibrium. The search for
stability and meaning finds its answer in the order of art, and the
two major themes of the earlier work, transvalued by the knowledge symbolized in the Marabar Caves, are reconciled at last.

Art and order are, naturally, not the only concerns of Forster's books (and they are not the only ones that will be treated
in this study), but they are primary to an understanding of
them and of what may be called Forster's world. They are the
clues to the exploration of what must otherwise remain too
large, craggy, and complex to grasp in its entirety. In setting out
to trace these through his work, then, the object of this study is
to present an **angle** of vision from which that world can be observed with some steadiness and clarity, an aid toward what
Forster has called "the sense of cooperation with a creator,
which is the supremely important step in our pilgrimage through
the fine arts" (*TC*, p. 117).

2 · The Aesthetic View of Life

1. WHERE ANGELS FEAR TO TREAD

Forster's first novel is his shortest, and the relative simplicity of its plot line makes it ideal for studying Forster's technique and intention. There are, to be sure, shuttlings back and forth between England and Italy, but the incidents of the story proceed in a straightforward fashion. There are few mysterious pockets to be turned inside out after the time of the incidents, no flashbacks to illuminate dark corners of the past. But there are surprise and suspense, and these constitute the second aspect of the plot, for, if the plot marches ahead with directness and speed, it experiences nonetheless certain startling moments along the route which make the journey no less straight, but considerably more intense. The plot is, in fact, in many respects melodramatic, and melodrama is a form congenial to Forster's way of looking at the world.

Melodrama, by its sudden highlighting of event, by its emphasis on the shocking, by its apparent disregard of the laws of cause and effect, provides a structural counterpart to what may be called Forster's philosophy of the great moment. If life is, as Forster seems generally to feel, essentially dull and, for most people at most times, meaningless, then it can derive significance only when some sudden burst of color illumines its gray surface. The eye accustomed to the steady, uninspired light of every day sees freshly only when it comes unexpectedly upon a virtual display of fireworks. So awakened, Forster's heroes think back upon the past, on into the future, trying as they do so to communicate to the drabness of ordinary life some of the glory that inheres in these great and infrequent moments. The anti-heroes have their eyes turned inward and see nothing at all. The melodramatic element of the plot is, furthermore, cousin to the fantasy of the stories. It provides the otherwise commonplace, realistic world of the novel with an atmosphere of strangeness; it pulls and tugs at the normal arrangement of things and leaves everything slightly disordered. Something odd, one feels, must be at work, disturbing the ordinary concatenation of events, but no cause can be found within the novel itself: there are no Pans or fauns, no Dryad or Siren just inside the woods or under the sea. Rather it is Forster at work, arranging and intensifying life so as to present a symbolic picture of what life is or should be.

The word "melodrama" suggests a theatrical metaphor, and such a metaphor is in fact appropriate to the book as a whole. If the plot provides the element of melodrama, the opposition between Italy and England provides the backdrop for the action, while Philip and Caroline are the actors downstage who most engage our attention. Italy and England (or Monteriano and Sawston) are sharply contrasted, and function as symbols of opposing ways of life. Philip and Caroline, on the other hand, are shifting and subtle figures, and the drama that takes place so largely in their minds becomes all the more significant by virtue of the decor behind them. The open air of the stories is here too, but it merges with the atmosphere of the theater, and in the central scene of the book huge gusts of spontaneity and joy of living rush through an opera house and almost sweep away its walls.

The contrast between Sawston and Monteriano provides, as does everything in the book, an opposition between the spectator's view of life and the ideal of active participation. *Where Angels Fear to Tread* gives a name and a definite location to that place from which come all the undesirable English of the short stories. Sawston is the England Forster does not like: its inhabitants are respectable, middle-class people; they are good in a conventional sort of way, full of the unconscious hypocrisy and petty unselfishness Forster stigmatizes in his essays. Appearances are essentially more important than the realities behind them, and life is a kind of mechanized game with seemingly important but actually trivial counters moving constantly in a meaningless round.

Mrs. Herriton, chief representative of Sawston in the book, puts all her energies into a vigorous pursuit of the outsides of things. Above all she enjoys power: her aim, as her son comes to recognize, is to repress vigor, and, as Forster points out, the keynote of her life is waste. Her daughter Harriet, physically unattractive and awkward, adherent to a rigid and unbeautiful evangelicism, is in some ways a much more attractive person, for however peevish and gloomy her creed may be, it is deeply felt. One of the virtues praised most strongly in the book is involvement. To stand on the sidelines of life is to be out of life, and Mrs. Herriton is always the director, never the actor.

Monteriano stands for Italy as Sawston does for England; within its walls are found all the qualities Mrs. Herriton and her sort lack. As in the short stories, Italy is not at all savage, "but it was terrible and mysterious all the same" (p. 65). The poetry that lies at the heart of things and that has at least one of its homes in Italy is not readily translatable into prose, but one of Philip's remarks about it helps explain its attraction for Forster: "People have lived so hard and so splendidly [here]" (p. 110), he says.

This hard and splendid living is most apparent at the opera already mentioned. The little theater is a microcosm of the Italian people and of the land in which they live. Philip and Harriet Herriton and their neighbor Caroline Abbott all attend a performance of *Lucia* on their first night in Italy, for though they have come to fetch away the Herritons' infant nephew from his father, Gino, whom they regard as a heathen (he is a Roman Catholic), there is nothing to be done this evening. There is time to look around before the opera begins: "So rich and so appalling was the effect, that Philip could scarcely suppress a cry. There is something majestic in the bad taste of Italy. . . . It observes beauty, and chooses to pass it by. But it attains to beauty's confidence" (p. 131).

The audience begins to tap and drum; Harriet emits a loud

"shish," and for a while the house is in order. "Her success annoyed [Philip]. He had grasped the principle of opera in Italy —it aims not at illusion but at entertainment—and he did not want this great evening-party to turn into a prayer-meeting. But soon the boxes began to fill, and Harriet's power was over" (p. 133). The opera house is a riot of uninhibited joy; feelings bubble up to the surface and spill over; there are no good manners to dampen spontaneity. Now the opera begins. Philip and Caroline fall into the spirit of the thing, but Harriet persists in trying to follow the plot. Everyone sways, the audience sounds drunk; someone throws a bouquet to Lucia, which she spins back into the audience, where it hits Harriet full in the chest. Harriet, righteously indignant, leads the English group out of the theater, and for her, though not for her companions, the evening ends as she had anticipated.

This is Forster's Italy at its best: music and laughter, high spirits bounding back and forth from stage to audience, art as a living force, as something shared, and majestic bad taste which "attains to beauty's confidence." Exuberance and enjoyment and honesty of feelings, these are the hallmarks of the Italians, and the Italian who best represents these qualities is Gino Carella, who stands in the same relation to Italy that Mrs. Herriton does to England. Gino functions primarily as the human embodiment of Forster's primitivist ideal; all of open-air Italy is his domain. Very much a part of his environment, he is beautiful and natural—or beautiful when he is natural, for he can be vulgar when he is trying to create an impression. His naturalness is most apparent in his feelings about his son. As his wife lies ill, ready to give birth, Gino worries terribly—but only secondarily about her. "Gino was distracted. She knew why: he wanted a son. He could talk and think of nothing else. His one desire was to become the father of a man like himself, and it held him with a grip he only partially understood, for it was the first great desire, the first great passion of his life. Falling in love was a mere physical triviality beside this divine hope of immortality: 'I continue' " (pp. 76–77).

Critics, particularly Professor Richards, have noticed the importance of this "continuance" theme throughout Forster's novels.[1] The passion that Gino feels is something elemental, something, we are led to believe, beyond understanding. It is, in a sense, a mark of Gino's physical quality and of his kinship with all things that spring up and grow in a natural manner. The feeling Gino experiences is for life itself, for something deeper not only than all the superficiality of Sawston, but deeper than his own individuality. Striving, as always, to find some unity beneath apparent chaos, Forster seeks to discover here something that binds all men together, and all men with nature. It is the supreme evidence of Gino's closeness to the heart of things that he feels this strongest of all desires.

The English, Harriet in particular, understand Gino's feeling only partially at best, and so conventional, misguided thinking wars against nature, and, when Harriet kidnaps the baby, it dies. Its death is symbolically the destruction of all hope of continuance and of meaning; nothing that follows quite cancels the effects of that event.[2] On Gino the death has, of course, an overwhelming effect. His attempted murder of Philip and, worse, his torture of him, follow insanely when he hears the news. Here is still another side of him: he is capable of violence, of cruelty, of brutal cunning. And yet, in the context of the story, all this is understandable. He acts under the stress of emotions which at the time are "natural"; he expresses in action all that he is feeling. If Forster appreciates more civilized behavior, he undoubtedly understands Gino's emotion and even can commend it in comparison with Mrs. Herriton's habitual repression of vigor and with the general tendency of the English to erect barriers between themselves and what is active or natural.

All of Gino's qualities—frankness and camaraderie with men, tenderness with his child, masterfulness with his wife, his exuberance, his brutality—comprise a whole and integral

1 See I. A. Richards, "A Passage to Forster: Reflections on a Novelist," Forum, LXXVIII (December, 1927), 914–20.
2 The baby at one point is compared with the infant Jesus. He is the hope of a better world, hope in the following generations, never fulfilled. Compare, too, Helen Schlegel's child in Howards End, below, chapter four, part one; and Stephen Wonham's in The Longest Journey, below, chapter two, part two; and the death of the unborn child in "The Story of the Siren," below, chapter three.

man. Even his external good looks reflect his enthusiasm and
vitality. He is in part Pan made human, in part Italy embodied.
Above all, he is dynamic, fully engaged in whatever he does, and
in this respect especially he functions as a measuring stick
against which the English must stand—in particular the tendency of Philip (and even of Caroline) to observe the human
scene as if it were a spectacle is to be contrasted with Gino's un-
stinting participation in that same scene. The actor and the
viewer come into conflict in the great theater that is Italy.

Philip's role of spectator is made apparent from the very
beginning of the book. Forster comments:

> At all events he had got a sense of beauty and a sense of
> humour, two most desirable gifts. The sense of beauty developed
> first. . . . At twenty-two he went to Italy with some cousins, and
> there he absorbed into one aesthetic whole olive-trees, blue sky,
> frescoes, country inns, saints, peasants, mosaics, statues, beggars.
> He came back with the air of a prophet who would either remodel
> Sawston or reject it. All the energies and enthusiasms of a rather
> friendless life had passed into the championship of beauty.
>   In a short time it was over. Nothing had happened either in
> Sawston or within himself . . . He concluded that nothing could
> happen, not knowing that human love and love of truth sometimes
> conquer where love of beauty fails.
>   A little disenchanted, a little tired, but aesthetically intact, he
> resumed his placid life, relying more and more on his second gift,
> the gift of humour. If he could not reform the world, he could at
> all events laugh at it, thus attaining at least an intellectual su-
> periority. (pp. 78–79)

That is Philip as the novel opens, laughing, not too attractively,
at everything around him. He finds Lilia's departure for Italy
whimsical and romantic, but Lilia's marriage to Gino puts an
end to his contented laughter. He leaves for Italy reluctantly and
confused. When Gino recites to him the opening lines of the
"Inferno," Forster comments that the "quotation . . . was
more apt than he supposed" (p. 38). It is Philip who is in the
dark wood and he has indeed lost the right path—or perhaps he
has never been on it. He is caught between his love for Italy
and his disinclination to have an Italian for a relative; England
and Italy fight within him, and the battle is all the harder since
Philip's Italy is as far from reality as is Sawston.

Disenchantment becomes even greater when Philip learns who his brother-in-law is, and greater still when he discovers that Gino's father is a dentist. "A dentist in fairyland! . . . he feared that Romance might die" (p. 32). Philip has been living in a world of make-believe, a painted world of which Forster does not approve. His idealization is false and is better gone. Forster comments: "Romance only dies with life. No pair of pincers will ever pull it out of us. But there is a spurious sentiment which cannot resist the unexpected and the incongruous and the grotesque. A touch will loosen it, and the sooner it goes from us the better. It was going from Philip now, and therefore he gave the cry of pain" (pp. 32–33).

It does not go completely, however—not yet. It is not until Philip's second trip to Italy, this time to "rescue" the baby, that he achieves as much liberation from the aesthetic view of life as he is able to attain. The significant turning point in Philip's development occurs at the opera. "He forgot himself as well as his mission. He was not even an enthusiastic visitor. For he had been in this place always. It was his home" (p. 134). What is there about the theater that makes it so appropriate a place for Philip's change, partial though it is, from viewer to doer? The opera house (as well as the Italy it represents) is where people can relate to one another—the actors to the audience, the audience to the actors and to each other, the English to the Italians. Although it is the home of art, "it aims not at illusion"; it is, indeed, completely antithetical to the frame of mind that so limits Philip's perceptions. The communication that has been so hard to achieve throughout the book is here possible. Italy breaks down barriers: its caffès and its opera houses open the way to relationships, and in Italy indeed all the English discover personal relations for the first time—all except Harriet, who although earnest, is not only English but religious. Significantly, it is she who receives the symbolic bouquet, the bouquet that sings, "Welcome! Join us! Be part of us!" Harriet's ability to communicate is cut off at the root; her muddle lies deeper beneath the surface than does her brother's. Lilia, Caroline, and Philip discover with varying degrees of success how to connect in Italy, for there, where the truth lies closer to the surface of things, men can reach across the abyss of loneliness and allow their fingers to touch.

And Philip's evening is not yet over. As Harriet leads the group from the theater, Gino leans over the balustrade of a box and extends the symbolic hand to Philip. The Englishman grasps it and finds himself rocketed up into a group of enthusiastic Italians. He is Fra Filippo, he is the guest of honor; he is happy now as he has never been. His sense of beauty, which had hitherto led him to look at life as all aesthetic surface, has now been conquered by "human love and love of truth." He has seen the true Italy, and he has glimpsed the possibilities of personal relations: the fantastic opera house, Gino and his friends have all begun to transform the friendless Sawstonian into a more vital human being. His enthusiasms will henceforth have more scope, and his life will have more meaning.

And yet Philip has not reached the final goal. When, the next day, Caroline asks him what he plans to do about the baby, he says he will speak to Gino and, should he fail, write home for more instructions, since, as he claims, he can understand the positions of all the interested parties. To Caroline's excited response that he must *do* something, he answers quietly and characteristically:

> "Some people are born not to do things. I'm one of them.
> . . . I never expect anything to happen now, and so I am never disappointed. You would be surprised to know what my great events are. Going to the theatre yesterday, talking to you now—I don't suppose I shall ever meet with anything greater. I am fated to pass through the world without colliding with it or moving it—and I'm sure I can't tell you whether the fate's good or evil. I don't die— I don't fall in love. And if other people die or fall in love they always do it when I'm just not there. You are quite right; life to me is just a spectacle, which—thank God, and thank Italy, and thank you—is now more beautiful and heartening than it has ever been before."
> She said solemnly, "I wish something would happen to you, my dear friend; I wish something would happen to you." (p. 168)[3]

---

3 In the course of his conversation with Caroline, Philip's "eyes rested agreeably on Santa Deodata" (pp. 165–66), whose picture is before him. The connection between Philip and the Saint is made several times in the book, for Deodata is the saint of the aesthetic view, who "in her death, as in her life . . . did not accomplish much" (p. 166).

Something, of course, does, and the passage is admirably ironic in its foreshadowing.[4] Soon after, the baby dies as Philip and his sister, with the boy on her lap, are thrown from their carriage, and Philip is himself almost killed by Gino.

As a result of the fight between the Englishman and the Italian, love, too, comes to Philip. Caroline, who "all through the day . . . had seemed to Philip like a goddess," stops Gino from killing him, and now, as Philip watches her comfort the sobbing man, he thinks:

Such eyes he had seen in great pictures but never in a mortal. . . . Philip looked away, as he sometimes looked away from the great pictures where visible forms suddenly became inadequate for the things they have shown us. He was happy; he was assured that there was greatness in the world. . . . Quietly, without hysterical prayers or banging of drums, he underwent conversion. He was saved. (p. 192)

Philip's conversion seems a fitting close to the novel, for the book is, in a sense, complete at this point. But there is one more chapter; Forster does not choose to end his *Bildungsroman* in quite the conventional way. That Philip—and Caroline—are by now better and more self-aware people there is no doubt, but Forster's faith in miraculous conversions is limited. On the train from Monteriano back to England, Philip realizes that "life was greater than he had supposed, but was even less complete" (p. 197). He experiences no joy because his human relations are not complete.

4 It is interesting to compare Forster with his hero. Philip, once he has shed his more offensive qualities, his snobbishness, his Sawstonian priggishness, is characterized above all by his spectator's view of life. Things are too complex, he says; he sees too easily all sides of a question. How can he act? How can he enter into the confusion of a world that he is able to view from all possible angles? One is reminded of Forster or, at any rate, of what Forster might have been, had some of his qualities been pushed to an excess. Indeed, Forster himself seems to have regarded Philip in that light. His hero, he has said, was modeled on Professor Dent, but, asked whether any of his characters represented himself, he singled out Philip as one of them. (See Furbank and Haskell, pp. 32–33.) Forster, too, is tentative, too hesitant to be dogmatic, and able to see life in its complexity. He believes, he has said in one of his essays, in faith with a little "f," but he does have a faith; Forster does act, does decide, does become involved. Philip is a Forster *manqué*, and undoubtedly that is one of the reasons for Forster's interest in him.

Caroline too seems lacking in real happiness; all the wonderful things are over, she thinks. Philip, who by now realizes that he is in love with her, thinks that at the root of Caroline's sadness lies an unstated love for himself. A strangely elliptical conversation takes place between them (Monteriano is already back in the past, and the difficulties of communication re-establish themselves), and from it emerges a bitter irony, for Caroline announces that she loves Gino and asks Philip—"because," as she says, "you're without passion; you look on life as a spectacle" (p. 201)—to laugh at her. Philip is forced to have thrown in his face what he thought to be his old dead self, a caricature of what he thinks he now is, and he realizes that it is his fault that all this has happened—that because his life was in danger Caroline came to see Gino again. Philip recognizes the irony of the situation and also its beauty and completeness. "For the thing was even greater than she imagined. Nobody but himself would ever see round it now. And to see round it he was standing at an immense distance" (pp. 203–4). Philip has the experience of a rich but lonely triumph, the awareness of something that cannot be communicated. And while Caroline continues to protest—"But all through [Gino] took me for a superior being—a goddess" (p. 204)—he hardly listens, for "his eyes were fixed on the Campanile of Airolo. But he saw instead the fair myth of Endymion. This woman was a goddess to the end" (p. 204).

There is something disquieting about the entire last episode. Neither Philip's feeling for Caroline nor hers for Gino rings true; both of them seem somewhat academic in their passion, for all their protestations of love. "And that saved me" (p. 204), Caroline says about Gino's attitude toward her, and one suspects that she is glad to have been saved. "What was the use of telling her?" thinks Philip, "For all the wonderful things had happened" (p. 204). It is not great passion that can be dampened so easily. Forster seems to be saying, in what constitutes a kind of epilogue to his book, that Philip and Caroline, despite their growth, have not been able to attain full stature, that the most difficult thing to achieve—true and lasting relationships and through them complete involvement in life—is not yet, perhaps never will be, within their grasp.

Philip, in his love for Caroline, takes a step back to his older, aesthetic way of looking at things: Caroline is a goddess and he regards her from afar. Even in the scene of his conversion his thoughts are of pictures, of art. He is focusing once again on the surface of things and overidealizing his love for woman as once he did his love for Italy. Furthermore, he resigns himself too easily to his defeat, as if defeat were in truth what he desired. His love is unreal precisely because it lacks sexual passion, or, more generally, vitality and body; it is weak and intellectual. Still, Forster is not presenting Philip as a failure, for he is said to grow by virtue of this sterile encounter. In fact, of all the characters in the book, he becomes most aware of life as it is: he is able to see around things, to understand the whole of the tangled relationships in the book. His love is fruitful, but as a means, not as an end; it contributes to his solitary growth. Truth wins out over love, but he will never again be a prig or a snob. What he is unable to conquer successfully is his most insistent enemy, his tendency to filter life through an aesthetic screen. The distance that such an attitude places between him and other people—the barrier it puts before the goal of love— seems to Forster to be the most difficult problem of all. To a degree Philip learns what is real in life, but he is never fully able to connect with it. The habit of idealizing and of seeing life as an artistic spectator prevents the final step of his education.

Caroline's love is no more real than Philip's; it, too, is an instrument of her growth, but it leads to nothing outside of herself, opens no doors to personal relations. It has its seat in her imagination, and one feels that she is probably glad it is so. Not only Philip, but Gino, too, regards Caroline as a goddess, and one wonders whether she herself is not to blame for the impression. To speak of her sexual impulses is as far as Caroline, still primarily under the domination of Sawstonian repressive forces, can or indeed wants to go. She tells Philip that she must speak to him of Gino from time to time or go mad; but her love, like Philip's, is a thing of art, not nature, and the verbal, not the physical, is the level on which she wants to keep it.

It says much about Forster's view of life as a whole that he should have chosen to end his book by exposing the inadequacy of his hero's and heroine's love. He seems, on the whole, to be indicating an essential sadness in life, a sadness that springs partly from the irony of circumstance, partly from the difficulty individuals experience in trying to make contact with the "real," partly from the difficulty inherent in the attempt to reconcile the claims of truth with love, of the aesthetic view with the giving of oneself in a relationship. Such a reconcilement may be possible in Italy, but in England and for the English it is more difficult. A gulf yawns before the feet of even the well intentioned. There is hope, Forster seems to say, but its fulfillment is sometime in the future; silence and loneliness are for the present. The last chapter gives a new direction to the book as a whole. The unreality of Philip's and Caroline's feelings makes the ending of the book more somber; the triumph that comes from their growth in self-knowledge is muted by their failure at interpersonal relations. The books ends, in fact, on the note of separation Forster was to recommend in his article "Pessimism in Literature" two years later.[5] The beauty of the myth of Endymion that comes to Philip's mind at the last is turned into irony, for it is the coldness and aloofness of the moon goddess that triumphs. Art wrests the final victory from nature, and education has still to be carried on, if possible.

2. THE LONGEST JOURNEY

At times a novelist fails to achieve sufficient distance from the problems that most interest him to use them as proper grist for his artistic mill. When that happens, the novel that results is likely to fail in coherence and integralness, but it may still be worth the reader's attention. It may in some ways become even more interesting to him, particularly in its tendency to reveal the conflicts that most beset its author. *The Longest Journey* is such a novel. Too much is attempted, too little resolved or even set forth clearly. The ambiguous word "reality" must be understood if the book is to be understood, and definitions, explicit and implicit, proliferate. Clearly what Forster has done is to project into his characters and their lives certain of

5 E. M. Forster, "Pessimism in Literature," *The Working Men's College Journal*, X (January, 1907), 6–10; X (February, 1907), 26–33.

the problems that most beset him, and what results is neither a set of solutions nor a complete vision of the world, but a dialectic of hope and despair carried on among several characters. Forster himself has invited an autobiographical reading of his novel: his leading character does many of the things Forster himself is known to have done, and Forster has said that "Rickie more than any" [1] of his characters represents himself.

This is not to say that *The Longest Journey* is thinly fictionalized autobiography, not, at any rate, in the conventional sense, for there are more differences than similarities between the external lives of Rickie and his creator. The novel is rather a spiritual biography of what Forster felt himself to be, what he thought he might become, and what he would like to have been. Forster has commented that he managed to get down in his novels only the people he admires, the people he dislikes, and the people he thinks he is,[2] and the formula is particularly applicable to this, his second novel. The characters are set one against the other and the novel is the arena in which they contend for the ultimate prize, the knowledge and possesion of what is most significant in life.

As might be expected, *The Longest Journey* carries on and elaborates many of the concerns that appeared in *Where Angels Fear to Tread*, and its hero, Rickie, another victim of the aesthetic view of life, embodies, now in a tragic context, many of the traits of Philip Herriton. Rickie, born in a suburb and therefore away from the redemptive powers of the country, is from the beginning aware of the grayness of the world and of the loneliness and incommunicability that exist among men. Afflicted with a twisted father, a reticent mother, and a limp which, in a book perhaps influenced by the philosophy of G. E. Moore,[3] is the external manifestation of an inner failure, Rickie is from childhood in large measure doomed: the wheels have already begun to grind slowly, and the rest unfolds with a certain inevitability. Public school gives to him only the desire to be left alone and the knowledge that "we are all of us bubbles

1 Furbank and Haskell, p. 33.
2 *Ibid.*, p. 32.
3 See Johnstone, Chapter II.

on an extremely rough sea. Into this sea humanity has built, as it were, some little breakwaters—scientific knowledge, civilized restraint—so that the bubbles do not break so frequently or so soon. But the sea has not altered" (pp. 67–68).

The experience of school, along with the early death of both his parents, makes clear to Rickie "the cruelty of Nature" (p. 217), but Rickie does not become bitter or pessimistic about his life. On the contrary, his longings for love and beauty become stronger. His character at this point combines a tremendous desire to find and make his own what is worthwhile in the world with an increasingly less effective awareness of the complexity of life. This awareness, while it lasts, gives depth and poignancy to his violent excursions into the realm of the imagination by pulling him sharply back to earth from each of his flights into that often deceptive realm.

Rickie enters Cambridge with a passionate yearning for beauty and personal affections, the two "goods" G. E. Moore had singled out for discussion in his *Principia Ethica*. Lame, physically and to some degree spiritually, he hopes to find fulfillment for his longings, preferably in objects fixed and stable that will front the waves of the surrounding sea. And for a time, at any rate, he does find them: Cambridge proves for him, as it did for Forster and many of his contemporaries, the home of friendships, of intellectual discussions, of poetry and philosophy, and of mingled earnestness and nonsense. Above all, unlike the public school from which he has come, his college, presumably King's, "though small, was civilized, and proud of its civilization" (p. 68). Here his cries for love and beauty are answered; here he discovers nature, Greece, England, and friends; here he turns writer. His eyes begin to open and he finds now at last proof that meaning and order do exist in the world.

And yet something is missing from Rickie's way of looking at things during these college years. He has forgotten the bubbles that break on the stream of life. In fact, Rickie at Cambridge is in many important ways similar to Philip in the final pages of *Where Angels Fear to Tread*. He has not the Sawstonian qualities that Philip learns to reject by the end of his experiences, but like him Rickie tends to view life at a distance:

his imagination, like Philip's, transforms experience into artistic configurations, recasting it into idealized shapes that no longer embody its fullness and flexibility. He is anxious, above all, to wrest order out of the chaos he has known, but he goes too far: he wishes to see fixity where there is none, and he sees meaning in life only by stepping back from it. He fails, therefore, to connect with the world and with the people who inhabit it. His relations with other people contribute solely to his own growth, not to the growth of the relationships themselves. But unlike Philip, he has no real conversion to undergo; he has within him already what he needs to make life successful.

The qualities that impede his success, that lead eventually to his ruin, are indicated, innocuously enough, in the opening scene of the book, in a conversation among a group of undergraduates gathered in the dark in Rickie's room. "It was philosophy. They were discussing the existence of objects. Do they exist only when there is some one to look at them? or have they a real existence of their own? . . . Is the cow there or not? This was better than deciding between objectivity and subjectivity" (p. 7). Thus the central problem of the book is announced, the problem of what is real.

Rickie and his friend Ansell—who, because he can instinctively recognize the truth, is our surest guide to Rickie's progress or decline—reveal their individual attitudes to life by their response to the question of the cow. 'She's there for me,' [Ansell] declared. 'I don't care whether she's there for you or not' (p. 7). Ansell has no doubt of what is real in any sense, and he does not hesitate to state his beliefs firmly and finally. But Rickie does not join the conversation; he finds it too difficult and his mind wanders.

Was she there or not? The cow. There or not. He strained his eyes into the night. Either way it was attractive. If she was there, other cows were there too. The darkness of Europe was dotted with them, and in the far East their flanks were shining in the rising sun. . . . Suddenly he realized that this, again, would never do. As usual, he had missed the whole point, and was overlaying philosophy with gross and senseless details. For if the cow was not there, the world and the fields were not there either. And what would Ansell care about sunlit flanks or impassable streams? (p. 8-9)

Ansell would not care, for Ansell is after Truth, but Rickie, as usual, begins to order and to transform into beauty whatever phenomena come before him. He is again framing life, as Philip did before him, so that it will remain forever hanging fixed on the wall of the inner, contemplative mind, undisturbed by the state of things as they are.

Into the midst of the conversation comes Agnes Pembroke, an acquaintance of Rickie, and the problem takes on more definite outlines. Throughout her stay, Ansell acts as if she were not there at all, and when Rickie upbraids him for his rudeness, he answers: "Did it never strike you that phenomena may be of two kinds: *one,* those which have a real existence, such as the cow; *two,* those which are the product of a diseased imagination, and which, to our destruction, we invest with the semblance of reality? If this never struck you, let it strike you now" (p. 24). Ansell then proceeds to draw a circle in a square, a square within that circle, and inside that another square. Rickie asks him if they are real, and to this Ansell responds: "The inside one is— the one in the middle of everything, that there's never room enough to draw" (p. 24).

Nothing as yet has been indicated about Agnes, and Ansell's behavior to her points up still more clearly his function in the novel. He has the power of apprehending whatever has value and of recognizing whether what he finds valuable corresponds to phenomenal reality. His power is almost mystical; it is immediate and infallible, and it is clear after the incident that Agnes is not, according to the values of the book, a real person: she is "not there." The incident is, of course, symbolic; it asks for the reader's concurrence in Ansell's judgment of Agnes, and it asks the reader to recognize Ansell's merits and Rickie's failings.

More important, the incident reveals the jumble of meanings that have been assigned to the word "real." The major problem of the book relates in some way to the proper understanding of reality, but how? The answer seems, at first sight, to concern the cow, for the novel opens with the undergraduate conversation. In fact, however, there is no doubt in the book about the reality of material phenomena. Ansell insists that the cow is there, and the old Berkeleian enigma is peacefully laid to rest; the epistemological problem is solved in the first pages, and the reader need not trouble further about the real in this sense.

Ansell, however, despite his assurance on this point, is disturbed by another aspect of the question of what is real, as it is symbolized in the metaphor of the circle and the square. What Ansell is seeking here is some ultimate meaning in the universe, something that, although it is presumably incapable of attainment, is in a sense the guarantee for all the values of the book. This phase of the problem is never made totally clear; the question is a metaphysical one and Forster does not solve it. Nonetheless the metaphor recurs from time to time in the course of the novel and adds a sense of mystery to it. In general what Ansell seems to be saying—and what Forster here seems to believe—is that one can discover meaning in the universe but that one cannot fathom the ultimate meaning— if there is one! One can approach it, but never reach it. Ansell knows this, but Rickie does not, and therein lies one explanation for his difficulties. He will come to feel that he *has* attained to the ultimate meaning, for it is always his desire to embody all that is good in one thing or person, to penetrate to the heart of the mystery.

More significant than either the cow or the circle and the square for the purposes of this novel are two other meanings Forster assigns to the word "real." Ansell gives the clue to these in his distinction between phenomena "which have a real existence" and those which are "the subjective product of a diseased imagination," a distinction that has particular reference to Rickie. A person who is unable to see material phenomena clearly as they *really* are (here the standard is Ansell in particular, but in general a common-sense apprehension of the ordinary world) is suffering from a psychological difficulty: his imagination is diseased, it invests everyday reality with subjective fancies. On the other hand, a person who is unable to determine which *values* are real is ethically deficient. The reader, when he encounters the word used in this way, should recall Forster's habitual distinction between the real and the pretended. A person may, of course, have values which are *personally* significant, but if they have no contact with objective reality, they are not *true* and will inevitably lead to tragedy. Now, the major problem of *The Longest Journey* is a psychological and ethical one, usually a combination of the two, and it is on this level that the book finds its true meaning. It is important henceforth to keep separate the various concepts that Forster lumps together in the word "real." Ansell, who is our guide in these matters, may be used to emphasize the point: he is able truly to apprehend *reality*, the world of phenomena (the psychological problem); he perceives what is *valuable* in the world (the ethical problem); and he is aware that behind the values he holds there exists some unattainable ultimate meaning (the metaphysical problem). The cow has done her work and need not be considered again.

Till now Rickie does hold the proper values and is, for the most part, able to keep them and his outlook in general from being merely subjective. At this point, though, his life becomes more and more bound up with Agnes, and it is because of his reaction to her that he begins a descent from the peak reached at Cambridge. During one of the Christmas vacations he visits her home and there finds Gerald Dawes, her fiancé, from whose bullying he had suffered at public school. He finds, as he thinks, that Agnes and Gerald do not love each other, that their lives are small and meaningless, and wonders whether he ought not to interfere to save Agnes from Gerald's rudeness and brutality. But something happens to change his mind. He comes upon the lovers in each other's arms and, for a moment, he watches and sees Agnes' face shine with "mysterious beauty" as Gerald kisses her. "He thought, 'Do such things actually happen?' and he seemed to be looking down coloured valleys" (p. 49). The "riot of fair images" that comes into Rickie's mind as he limps away marks the end of his ability to see things as they really are, for his vision corresponds not to the lovers themselves but to his conception of what lovers ought to be.

The scene recalls Philip as he watched Gino in Caroline's arms, the scene from which Philip averted his eyes as from great pictures. Philip looking at life through the distorting mirror of art, Philip creating a goddess of Caroline, Philip putting distance between himself and life: Philip or Rickie, the reactions are the same, the objects in Rickie's case far less worthy. He has imposed order on the chaotic world he wishes not to see, and the image once created is fixed forever: "They had got into heaven, and nothing could get them out of it" (p. 50).[4] Agnes in particular is transfigured by him; he is Swann to her Odette. "He smiled at the idea of her being 'not there.' . . . She had more reality than any other woman in the world" (p. 57).

Gerald's sudden death—one of the book's "moments"— makes it easy for Rickie now to transfer his feelings to Agnes alone, and indeed Agnes herself helps to overcome his scruples. More assertive than Rickie, she takes the lead in bringing about a formal engagement, and his love has finally found a definite embodiment. As Ansell comments about his friend: "He is happy because he has at last hung all the world's beauty on a single peg. He was always trying to do it. He used to call the peg humanity" (p. 94). Rickie has embarked unwittingly on the longest journey of the title, and henceforth his path is a dreary one, for he has chosen not the most perfect woman in the world but an unworthy and jealous foe.

Agnes' destructive influence on Rickie becomes apparent even before their marriage, when Stephen Wonham enters his life and Rickie is offered a symbolic moment, one of those moments, according to Forster, at which a man must cease to drink from the teacup of experience and become an experience himself. The reader knows little about Stephen so far, but it is soon clear that for Forster he is the value center of the book. Rickie's reactions are quite different, for he finds the boy vulgar and boorish. Once, Forster says, Rickie would have been attracted by fresh people: "then they had been to him symbols of the unknown, and all that they did was interesting. But now he cared for the unknown no longer. He knew" (p. 124). He knows, that is to say, that all that can be known is to be found in Agnes. Rickie, we are meant to feel, has missed seeing what

---

4 The passage represents, it seems, a deliberate attempt to show the falsity of Rickie's perceptions, not an example of Forster's purple prose, as a number of recent critics seem to feel. See, for example, W. J. Harvey, "Imagination and Moral Theme in E. M. Forster's *The Longest Journey*," *Essays in Criticism*, VI (October, 1956), 431; and J. B. Beer's answer in his *The Achievement of E. M. Forster* (New York: Barnes & Noble, 1962), pp. 86–88. See also Crews, p. 58.

is essential in Stephen. Up to now his failure has been one of perception; he has been unable to see that, in his love of Agnes, he has constructed a purely subjective idol. But once he takes Agnes as the perfect example of all that is good, his values begin slowly but inevitably to change. Consequently, his misjudgment of Stephen has an ethical, as well as a psychological basis; Rickie, who has hitherto valued the inner man, is satisfied now to make decisions on the basis of the outer man alone.[5]

Shortly after this meeting, Rickie learns from Mrs. Failing, his aunt and Stephen's guardian, the true identity of the boy. A stupid and trivial argument takes place between Rickie and the older woman, and the cynical Mrs. Failing, who dislikes being contradicted, blurts out that Stephen is his brother. Rickie faints and wakes to find himself being revived by Stephen. The moment is crucial; he may yet find meaning in a person who is really good and set straight his perceptions by acknowledging Stephen: "there broke from him a cry, not of horror but of acceptance. For one short moment he understood. 'Stephen—' he began, and then he heard his own name called: 'Rickie! Rickie!' Agnes had hurried from her post on the margin, and, as if understanding also, caught him to her breast" (p. 151). The moment passes; like a huge cloud, subjective delusion and muddle in the form of Agnes obscure the brightness of truth that, we are to believe, is Stephen's.

So Rickie completes the first stage of his journey. The Cambridge years are over and his closest link is with Agnes. Now that his faulty perceptions, his diseased imagination, have begun to affect his values, he is ready to follow the path to Sawston, home of the Pembrokes and of the Herritons in *Where Angels Fear to Tread.* There his closest association is with Herbert Pembroke, his brother-in-law, a schoolmaster of a lower form in the Sawston public school. Herbert is an organizer, a lover of

---

5 Of course, the reader, too, has probably missed seeing anything in Stephen deserving particular esteem: the encounter has been symbolically right (as the rest of the book proves), but realistically wrong, and the reader must accept Forster's word when he says that a few months before Rickie would have seen something other than vulgarity. We know that Rickie's perceptions have become slovenly and that his values have begun to deteriorate, but so far we must accept Stephen's better qualities on trust.

method for method's sake; his life is spent in a colossal waste of effort, for he never manages to penetrate to the heart of any matter. His passion for order is in a way a parody of Rickie's, since it exists on a different level; Rickie is motivated by an awareness of the surrounding darkness, whereas Herbert is aware of nothing outside of Sawston. All his organizing is, consequently, completely barren. Not unnaturally, his mind is enormously attracted by facile analogies: school is the world in miniature; it is a microcosm of the great outside about which Rickie, too, has begun to be confused. For Rickie, tradition is of incalculable importance because it represents a natural connection with the past. Herbert, on the other hand, is anxious to impose tradition, to pretend that that which has never been exists.

Despite his awareness of Herbert's philistinism and stupidity, Rickie is sucked into the Sawstonian way of life. Excited at first about teaching, he loses his first enthusiasm, finds it easier to be severe, and becomes a martinet. Gradually he comes to accept the arrangements of Dunwood House, of which Herbert is master, although his first reaction to them is unfavorable. Even his marriage proves a disappointment and, as Rickie comes to know Agnes better, the relationship degenerates into one of superficial good-fellowship. Obscurely he realizes that something is wrong and he prays "to be delivered from the shadow of unreality that had begun to darken the world" (p. 173), but he does not know how to remove the shadow himself. Henceforth the reader's sympathy for Rickie is of a kind different from what it was before: it is based partly on a remembrance of his better self, partly on the awareness that from time to time Rickie still has glimmerings of understanding of what is happening to him. On the whole, however, Rickie becomes a less admirable person. Not only his perceptions are at fault now, for although he continues to transform others, he also loses his own awareness of what is valuable. Rickie has become a Sawstonian.

Only one thing now makes Rickie feel he still has some idea of what is valuable in life. His wife is about to have a baby:

It dawned on him, as on Ansell, that personal love and marriage only cover one side of the shield, and that on the other is graven the epic of birth. In the midst of lessons he would grow dreamy, as one who spies a new symbol for the universe, a fresh circle within the square. . . . Here is meaning of a kind. . . . He would forget himself in his son. (p. 207)

This time Rickie feels, not that he has "the" answer, that he is about to attain to the ultimate meaning, but that he has discovered a new aspect of it. Here he is at one with Ansell; he has a glimpse of things truer than those with which he has been living for the last months.[6] For Rickie, hope lies with his child. But the child is born with his own affliction and soon dies. Now his unstable world falls completely to pieces. Agnes, like the world she has created for him, has no meaning any more. "He remained conscientious and decent, but the spiritual part of him proceeded towards ruin" (p. 218). Rickie has reached the end of the road along which he has been making the longest journey.[7] All, it seems, is over with his noble aspirations, his fair dreams, and so it is, in so far as he has control over his own destiny, but now Ansell and Stephen re-enter his life, and for a while the shadow of unreality passes.

Ansell searches through a good part of the novel for an adequate embodiment of the values he is able instinctively to recognize, and this he finds in Stephen when he meets him for the first time in the garden of Rickie's house. Ansell has previously told a friend who accused him of being too intellectual, "When the moment comes I shall hit out like any ploughboy"

6 The curious undertone of the book recurs here: love is so important in the book's code of values, and yet personal love and marriage are only one side of the shield. It is implied that the other is the truer side, the side that represents birth. It is interesting to note how alone Forster's characters are when their great moments come. A quasi-mystical communion with the as yet unborn seems more significant than relations with other men and women. Rickie seems about to escape from the muddle of his relations not by establishing better communications with other human beings but by communing in solitude with something that is natural. Only solitude brings the awareness of order; the barriers to understanding others, Forster sometimes feels, are too great.

7 There is no doubt that Forster shares with his hero an attraction to the aesthetic view of life, and that in this book he is fighting against it at least in part in his treatment of Rickie. This explains, perhaps, why Rickie so often seems the victim of some preordained plot. There is never more than temporary respite for Rickie; for Forster he is damned from the beginning.

(p. 204). He is watching, he says, for the Spirit of Life, and at Sawston he seems to see it in Rickie's brother. Their meeting, which begins with a fight and ends with a friendship, enables Ansell to connect, as he has not before, Truth with Love and Beauty. To Ansell, Stephen, a true son of Demeter, "gave the idea of an animal with just enough soul to contemplate its own bliss" (p. 239), and Ansell very much likes the animal quality he sees in him. In effect he finds in Stephen almost the opposite of what he himself is. Whereas Stephen presumably embodies the same Spirit of Life he has till now found in books, one suspects that Ansell is attracted by Stephen's total lack of any quality suggesting museums or reading rooms. To Agnes he announces that he has had "a momentary contact with reality" (p. 251), and the effects of that contact are soon apparent. Having learned of Stephen's relationship to Rickie and believing that Rickie is unaware of it, he tells him of his brother and accuses Agnes of dishonesty. When he discovers that Rickie does indeed know but thinks Stephen is his father's son, he denounces him to the assembled school and tells him that his brother is his mother's child. Rickie collapses and is carried from the room.

Now begins the last scene in the tragic drama of Rickie's life. He is horrified to learn that Stephen is his beloved mother's son and the revelation leaves him spiritually bankrupt. It is Ansell who helps him to purge himself of remorse and guilt, to see his mother and Stephen with clearer eyes. He no longer feels Stephen is inherently bad; in fact, he begins to reshape his values so that now, once again, he is closer to being able to understand what is good. But the transformation of his values cannot be completed. The seeds of destruction that seem to take perpetual root in Rickie begin almost immediately to grow, and even now he starts to idealize Stephen, to separate the meaning that he, unlike Agnes, does have, from the other elements of his personality. He cannot look quite straight at Stephen, who is *not* perfect, for the image of his mother is in the way.

Stephen himself recognizes that this is so, for when Rickie, portrait of their mother in hand, goes to his brother to ask him to live with him, Stephen tears the portrait to bits. "I see your game," he tells him. "You don't care about *me* drinking, or to shake *my* hand. It's someone else you want to cure—as it were, that old photograph" (p. 283). Rickie realizes suddenly that Stephen is right. Rickie does not love him, just as he never hated him; in either case Stephen was merely a symbol. Stephen says, however, that he has no objection to Rickie coming with him—as a man, not as a brother. Rickie hesitates for only a moment: "The words were kind; yet it was not for their sake that Rickie plunged into the impalpable cloud. In the voice he had found a surer guarantee" (p. 286). The voice Rickie hears is his mother's, and in following it he is following what seems to be the surest order he has yet been able to find in the world, the order that comes from the natural links between one generation and another, the order that is the racial essence.

In accompanying his brother, Rickie does, in effect, the right thing for the wrong reason. He and Stephen go to live with Ansell, and soon Rickie is in all ways so much more stable and happy that, when Mrs. Failing asks him to visit her, he goes, although he knows that she wants to speak to him about Agnes. He allows Stephen to accompany him on the trip but extracts the promise that he will give up drinking. Rickie visits his aunt alone and, as expected, Mrs. Failing urges him to return to his wife. Rickie tells her he does not love Agnes; she knows that, Mrs. Failing answers, but the conventions are important. We do not live for great passions or for great memories or for great anything, she continues. Beware of the earth, she insists. "Beware of her surely. Going back to her really is going back—throwing away the artificiality which (though you young people won't confess it) is the only good thing in life" (p. 304). But Rickie knows better now. The world is real again, he thinks.

Mrs. Failing goes to bed, warning her nephew again about the earth, but Rickie goes out to look for Stephen. Thinking to himself that Stephen is a hero, a law to himself, he walks down to the village. There he discovers that Stephen is drunk. He is incredulous; Stephen wouldn't break his promise! But he has, and Rickie is crushed; he is bankrupt again. "May God receive me and pardon me for trusting the earth" (p. 311), he prays. Again Rickie has failed to perceive reality correctly; his subjective delusion has been smashed to pieces by concrete fact. And again his values have become corrupt, for he has allowed

Stephen's momentary behavior (for which there are, in any case, extenuating circumstances) to take precedence over the real and abiding value of the man. Meanwhile Stephen has left the inn where he had been, and Rickie finds him lying unconscious across some railroad tracks. A train is approaching, and wearily Rickie saves his brother's life and tries to save his own, but the train goes over his knees. He dies at his aunt's house, whispering to her, "You have been right" (p. 312).

But Mrs. Failing is not right; Rickie dies, not because he has trusted the earth, but because he has not trusted it enough.[8] He has never been more muddled than at the moment he dies, when he returns once more to an artificial view of life, the view that demands unreal and impossible perfection. In fact the earth is good and Stephen is good, but neither the one nor the other is unchanging or perfect; life and art have been confused again. Rickie's death is almost unbearably pathetic, for he is unaware of the tragic irony of all he says; there is no moment of illumination before the end. The preordained wretchedness of his life, symbolized from the beginning by his limp, comes to an end with symbolic fitness as the train crushes both his legs. Only death itself helps alleviate the pathos, for it is better, at any rate, than the prospect of Rickie dragging his exhausted body back into the darkness of the Sawstonian night. The road he has traveled has led, again and again, to an ever foggier apprehension of what is valuable in life. His search for perfect order has led to the ultimate disorder, to chaos, to death. It is in the end as it was in the beginning: Rickie has passed through life never having managed to make contact with the earth or its people, never having managed to connect his vision with reality.

But the book does not, or is not meant to, end as depressingly as Rickie himself, for Stephen remains. If Forster has condemned Rickie, and that in himself which is Rickie, to inevitable death and failure, he still has hope for a better way of life, for an answer to the failures of the aesthetic vision. Stephen

8 See Reuben A. Brower, "Beyond E. M. Forster, Part I—The Earth," *Foreground*, I (Spring–Summer, 1946), 170–71, for a different interpretation of this incident.

is a hero for Forster, too, and in some ways Forster's admiration is no less fatal for his book than was Rickie's for him. Rickie remains the protagonist of the novel, but Stephen is its ideal, and with him lies whatever final answer there is.

Stephen is the child of poetry and romance, of a union between Rickie's mother and a farmer who had a passionate love for the earth. His father dies only days after he leaves the country with Mrs. Elliot, and she dies while he is a child, so Stephen is entrusted to the care first of Mr. Failing and then of Mrs. Failing.[9] The old woman is bored by Stephen as a boy, missing in him the romance she feels should be his—but, as Forster comments, "he lived too near to the things he loved to seem poetical" (p. 269). So he grows up in his own way, riding, bathing, and working as and when he likes, crude externally but something better inside. Forster describes him on the brink of manhood: "His parents had given him excellent gifts—health, sturdy limbs, and a face not ugly—gifts that his habits confirmed. They had also given him a cloudless spirit— the spirit of the seventeen days in which he was created" (p. 269). He is still immature, and even something of a bully, but he is not petty and vindictive like Gerald Dawes. He is more like Gino of *Where Angels Fear to Tread* in his vigorous response to life, in his essential honesty, and in his oneness with nature. In his room hangs a single picture, the Demeter of Cnidus, the earth mother who watches over him. Not that Stephen worships the forces of nature in any conscious way. Mrs. Failing mistakes him when she tries to make him out a modern pagan. Her own attitude to the earth is severely aesthetic, but Stephen's is quite different. His connection with Demeter, or with what she represents, is instinctive: for him, as for his parents before him, the earth resembles a living being, and, like his father, he enjoys strenuous contact with it. Stephen belongs in the country. Even his bastardy in some ways sym-

9 It often happens in Forster's novels that one individual must die in order that another may live; even continuity, the natural order, is not a perfect order. Could children love their parents as their parents love them, Forster says in *Where Angels Fear to Tread*, all might be different, but Forster does not believe after all that things can be different, and, unwilling to give voice to disillusionment, he removes the possibility of contact between father and son and between mother and son.

bolizes his "naturalness," his closeness to the earth; he is the embodiment of nature made human.

When Stephen is forced to leave Cadover, therefore, it is as if a plant were uprooted from its native soil. His return to Wiltshire, when he accompanies Rickie, marks the beginning of a change for him, a change in the direction of greater stability and maturity. Rickie notices Stephen's excitement as they sight the spire of Salisbury Cathedral, but Stephen is more excited still by the country around; he has returned to his roots, to his tradition. *The Longest Journey* is filled with love for the country-side, particularly for the English countryside, and though Rickie loves England, it is Stephen who lives close to its land and makes part of its history. That this is so is shown most beautifully in an incident that occurs as the two boys pass a stream. Stephen wades in and asks Rickie for matches; he takes a piece of paper and crumples it into a ball.

The paper caught fire from the match, and spread into a rose of flame. "Now gently with me," said Stephen, and they laid it flower-like on the stream. Grave and tremulous weeds leapt into sight, and then the flower sailed into the deep water, and up leapt the two arches of a bridge. "It'll strike!" they cried; "no it won't; it's chosen the left," and one arch became a fairy tunnel, dropping diamonds. Then it vanished for Rickie; but Stephen, who knelt in the water, declared it was still afloat, far through the arch, burn-ing as if it would burn for ever." (p. 302)

All the water imagery of the novel comes together here. What for Rickie had always been turbid waters on which floated perishable bubbles is for Stephen a gentle stream lit by a mystic fire far into the future. Rickie is destined never to have children, but he knows that Stephen will, that "through his remote posterity, [he] might be mingled with the unknown sea" (p. 217). Stephen is of the stuff that does survive; his remotest ancestors, men and women of the soil, live through him, and he will live in his descendants forever, passing on the racial purpose that manifests itself in him.

Rickie's death follows shortly after the scene at the stream, but the book is not over. As was the case in *Where Angels Fear to Tread*, there is a final chapter that serves as a kind of epilogue, and in it one learns that Stephen is a farmer now and married,

that "his manners were growing rough, for he saw few gentle-
men now, and he was either incoherent or else alarmingly direct" (p. 316). In his house hang two pictures: one of Stock-
holm, where his mother had fled with her lover (a picture that
had been Rickie's), and the other of the Demeter of Cnidus.
"Outside the sun was sinking, and its last rays fell upon the
immortal features and the shattered knees" (p. 318), knees
shattered like Rickie's own and suggesting that he shares vicari-
ously in some way in Stephen's life. That he does so is made
still clearer in what follows. Stephen goes out of doors with his
daughter, and, as the child falls asleep, he thinks:

He had always been grateful, as people who understood him knew.
But this evening his gratitude seemed a gift of small account. The
ear was deaf, and what thanks of his could reach it? . . . The spirit
had fled, in agony and loneliness, never to know that it bequeathed
him salvation. . . . One thing remained that a man of his sort
might do. He bent down reverently and saluted the child; to whom
he had given the name of their mother. (p. 320)

Stephen's gratitude, as he himself realizes, is of little account. Rickie is dead in spirit as well as in body. His niece
carries his beloved mother's name, but to the end he himself
is his father's son; in no real way will he participate in the generations that are to follow. Rickie's ultimate failure, however,
had been inevitable and need not be dwelt upon. What is significant is to determine whether Stephen's final triumph counter-
balances, as it is intended to do, Rickie's defeat, whether the
answer he presents to the aesthetic view of life compensates for
the values that are never realized in Rickie's life and that die
with him. Forster clearly is setting against one another the two
ways of life represented by Rickie and by Stephen, and the
epilogue shows Stephen's to be victorious. The question remains
whether the reader is convinced or satisfied, and the answer
seems to be that he is not.

One reason for the reader's dissatisfaction lies with Forster's presentation of Stephen, who functions on two levels, a
realistic one and a symbolic one. On the realistic level Stephen
remains to the end somewhat childish and clumsy, decidedly
unintellectual; on the symbolic level he is meant to be nothing
less than the poetry at the heart of the world, the answer to all

the problems that are raised in the book. But Forster, very much like Rickie, never manages fully to connect what is of value with what is real. One might almost imagine that, had Rickie written a novel, he would have written *The Longest Journey*, and that he would have continued to overidealize Stephen to the very end of the book.

Of greater significance than this technical fault, however, is the more important and fundamental one that has to do with Forster's conception of Stephen. That Forster, in an earlier draft of his novel, named him Siegfried.[10] says something of the way in which he conceived him: he is, notwithstanding the fact that Rickie goes wrong by regarding his brother as a hero, cast in the heroic mold. His value comes out most clearly in the way in which he is opposed to other characters in the book, particularly to Rickie. In fact, what Rickie searches for, Stephen is, for Stephen has behind him the unconscious wisdom of his farmer-ancestors, whereas Rickie, like his aunt and his father, is, so to speak, "artificial." In various ways all three of the Elliots respond to life at second hand, through the medium of art: Mrs. Failing sees Nature aesthetically; Mr. Elliot acts as if life were a play; while Rickie, as author, husband, and brother, refashions all experience into a lovely and enduring picture. Stephen is not only contrasted with his brother, he is a test for him as well. Rickie must recognize and accept the "reality" of Stephen, as Ansell does, if he is to overcome his weaknesses and live successfully. He cannot meet the challenge; he fails and dies.

In contrast to the intellectual and emotional sterility of Sawston and of Rickie, Stephen is meant to represent fertility, growth, life, and so, inevitably, continuity. Of all the searches for order that occur in the book—Rickie's desire for fixity and permanence, Herbert Pembroke's passion for organization, Ansell's search for what lies within the final circle or the final square—only Stephen's is successful, for he fulfills himself through that order that connects man most closely with nature itself. Ansell is unmarried, Rickie's baby dies, and only Stephen

10 Furbank and Haskell, p. 31.

perpetuates himself: his is the one order that is not imposed. But has not Forster dropped some values along the way? Does Stephen really make up for the loss of the values that were Rickie's? Rickie, it must be remembered, is, for all his faults, a sincere lover of the intellect, of books, of poetry, of Cambridge; and this world, it would seem, is closed to Stephen. As a symbol of opposition, Stephen is significant; as something positive in himself, he is far less adequate. Furthermore, one may ask whether Stephen succeeds in overcoming the silence, the loneliness, the incommunicability that are so much a part of the book's mood. He does not manage ever to connect, to relate to other people. In effect, the only connection he makes is with the generations behind him and, through his daughter, with the generations to come, but even here the connection is more symbolic than real. Of his marriage, of his wife, we hear virtually nothing, and the reader is less and less convinced of Stephen's solidity on any level at all.

Whether or not Forster did consciously feel these things, the fact remains that the book ends with a vision of hope still further removed. Stephen's child is the future, and the last chapter focuses on her. It is as if Forster wished still more meaning than Stephen embodies, or as if he felt that no one man was able to encompass all that is good. Beyond the circle and the square there still remains mystery, for the baby represents not only the fulfillment of man's greatest and most primitive urge, but also hope deferred. Rickie dies so that the baby may live; Stephen passes on to her the spirit of the generations. And yet, the child as she appears in the book is without character, without personality—she is symbol and no more. Perhaps, like the child that is never born in "The Story of the Siren," she will at last overcome silence and loneliness; perhaps with her (although one does not really believe this) connection will at last be achieved. Hope lies in the unseen future, since the present is, after all, for all the characters in the novel, a long and solitary journey. The dialectic of Forster's mind continues: despair breeds hope, not today, but possibly tomorrow, and from the sad ashes of all these unconnected lives perhaps Stephen's child will arise, a phoenix, to glimpse a better day.

3. A ROOM WITH A VIEW

In many ways *A Room with a View* is Forster's best-controlled and most perfectly realized piece of work. In scale and intention it is slighter than some of the other books, but in what it sets out to do it succeeds almost completely. Forster is, for the first time, entirely at ease with his material. *A Room with a View* was in fact the first novel Forster began, but, as he has said, after he had got half way through, there was some hitch.[1] The hitch probably resulted from Forster's inability to extricate himself sufficiently from the problems that constitute the major themes of the first two novels to set them in comic relief. For *A Room with a View*, which revolves about those same themes, was planned as a comic work in 1903, and Forster had apparently to put it aside until 1908, by which time he had expressed and at least partially removed the urgent seriousness from those questions that preoccupied him most.

A *Room with a View* is in a sense, then, a coda to the novels that precede it: its concerns are similar, but its manner and point of view are different. It is the only one of the five novels in which an attempt is made to bring about a happy ending through the agency of true love. The major theme of the novel, as of the earlier ones, is expressed in the contrast between two opposed responses to life: the one, direct and vigorous; the other, vicarious and guarded. But this opposition, which can be resolved into the distinction between what is natural and what is artificial, is handled in a new way here. The aesthetic view of life is still a problem in the book, but it is now an external rather than an internal threat to the protagonists. It is the minor characters who are the spectators of life, and for the most part they are treated as subjects for laughter and satire. Forster's more optimistic attitude is most apparent in the fact that his hero and heroine are ultimately capable of complete redemption and that they stand at the last among the exemplars of the natural life.

The basic contrast of the book is repeated in many ways.

---

1 Furbank and Haskell, p. 31.

In fact, the novel operates in large measure by a technique that is not new to us, an opposition, constantly repeated, of one set of values against another. At times the country is set against the city, the Renaissance against the Middle Ages, deep religious feeling against formalized religion; still more obviously the opposition is expressed in terms of imagery, as when light, air, and a view are contrasted with darkness, closeness, and density. Even the characters act as obvious foils to one another and so intensify the background of sharp conflict against which the protagonists move. But it is by attending to the two images (apart from that of the view) that recur most frequently in the book that one can best understand the feeling the book as a whole conveys. On the one hand, there is the image of a battle: characters are constantly girding themselves or entering into hostilities, so that one has the impression of armies of good and bad marshaled for war. On the other hand, there is the image of water, never here, as in *The Longest Journey*, an awful and threatening ocean, but a friendly stream, a small pool, a rivulet of flowers. Herein lies that part of the novel which makes for merging, for continuity, for the softening of the hostility that comes from the struggle between systems of values. That the water will wash away all traces of battle is apparent from the beginning; the reader of *A Room with a View* enjoys the excitement of conflict along with the assurance of victory.

The world of *A Room with a View* has Lucy Honeychurch as its center, and all the pieces fall into place when Lucy comes to understand herself and the people around her. As heroine, Lucy stands somewhere between the Victorian young lady and Wells's Ann Veronica or the heroines of Shaw. She is conscious both of her predecessor and of the "New Woman," but she is not quite either. On the whole she is most like Evelyn Beaumont of "Other Kingdom," who, like Lucy, has little desire for a room of her own, but very real longings to possess her own soul or, at least, to share it on terms of equality with the man she loves.

Lucy is probably the most fortunate of Forster's leading characters as far as her family and her home, Windy Corner, are concerned. She and her family and her house are permanent as nature is permanent; they are to some extent part of nature.

Things at the Honeychurch household proceed in an unpremeditated but (or, perhaps, therefore) successful way. The Honeychurches are not completely free of philistinism, but the charge is unimportant for Forster. More important, they are not prigs; they do not pretend to have feelings or tastes which are not theirs, and they are, above all, spontaneously affectionate. Their lives take form, somehow, from within them, from things they would be unable to explain, but that are nonetheless vital and important.

As the book opens Lucy has for the first time left her home and come face to face with a new culture, with new people, with new ways of looking at the world. She has traveled, with her cousin Charlotte as chaperon, to Italy, and one can anticipate the effect of Forster's Italy on one of Forster's English. In fact, left to herself, Lucy manages to discover or intuit what is right and wrong, but, unfortunately, in Florence she has little time to be alone. From the first, her impulses are smothered or rationalized away by her cousin, who serves as contrast to and bad influence upon her. It is Charlotte who first refuses and then accepts with bad grace the offer to exchange rooms made by the Emersons, fellow tourists at their pension who have rooms with views. It is Charlotte throughout who suggests fog and thick curtains, closed spaces and dense air.

Without quite realizing why she feels as she does, Lucy tries constantly to keep herself from being enveloped by her cousin. The Emersons, particularly young George, try to dissipate Charlotte's fog with their view, and they present Lucy with her first challenge to be herself and to follow her own instincts. George himself is, at least through most of the book, a more reflective individual than Lucy, and because his father senses but does not understand the inner disturbance to which George's thought gives rise, he asks Lucy to help him: "Make my boy think like us. Make him realize that by the side of the everlasting Why there is a Yes—a transitory Yes if you like, but a Yes" (p. 38). The Emersons, father and son, are agnostics of the first and second generation; believing essentially the same things, they are, by temperament, completely different. Mr. Emerson's attitude, despite his materialism and his philosophic pessimism, has the fundamental assurance of a religious outlook.

His mind has made what sense it could of the world, of the Why, and has gone on to focus on what to him is the more important problem, the transitory Yes. But George is more interested, or disturbed, by the Why; unable simply to accept the knot in the eternal smoothness, he wishes to understand it. His is the search for order in the novel, the attempt to make sense of the chaos he feels around him.

As the book goes on Lucy becomes more and more the answer for George, just as he becomes a test for her. Throughout, even when they seem most apart, each is subtly present to the other, as the fulfillment of a desire or as an irritating reminder of an unacknowledged truth. Their first significant contact occurs a few days after Lucy's arrival at the pension. Having spent some time buying photographs of famous statues and paintings, Lucy wanders into the Piazza Signoria and there witnesses a murder. As she faints, George Emerson, who has been standing nearby, comes to her rescue, and when she recovers she finds herself in his arms. Embarrassed as she is, Lucy immediately tries to appear nonchalant, and the significance of the death is not immediately apparent. It becomes clear, however, in a symbolic incident that follows. The two young people walk to the Arno, and there Lucy sees George throw something into the river. Suddenly she recalls the pictures, and indeed, as it turns out, George has flung the blood-stained photographs away: art (the photographs: life arranged and formally stabilized) must give way before real life, as revealed by the suddenness of death. As in the other novels, so here, a sudden moment focuses all the confusion of daily life and focuses it in a "natural" way.

George, because of this event, begins to feel that perhaps there is meaning in the tangle of the universe, and in some way his desire to live now involves the desire to know Lucy better. He has begun to feel love, which, as his father says, "is one of the moments for which the world was made" (p. 248), and which in *A Room with a View* is the most important value. Lucy, on the other hand, shows that she is not yet able to get the best out of herself, that she is unable to follow her good impulses. She refuses George's obvious though unstated request to continue their relationship and tries to pretend that nothing of significance has happened. George is disturbed, but Lucy is frightened, and she is frightened largely because she is unable to forget the precepts of respectability so wearisomely exemplified by her cousin. For the moment she puts life at a distance, as Charlotte would do, rather than facing it directly in the manner of George.

The next important moment for George and Lucy comes as a result of an outing organized by the resident English chaplain, the offensive Mr. Eager, but presided over by the god Pan. Fantasy is most prominent in the novel in the scene devoted to the outing, for here various levels of reality meet and mingle and have their effect on the English—although no one of them, least of all Lucy, understands completely what is happening. Deeper than the interpersonal clashes that Forster records in the spirit of social comedy, there is a battle within Lucy's heart, and around her and George operate the forces of Italy and of still more distant myths. Their carriage is driven by Phaethon and beside him sits Persephone; the party is being conducted by the forces of love, of spring, and of the earth.

And Phaethon does more than drive the carriage, for when later in the day Lucy goes looking for the two chaplains of the party, she approaches the young man and asks him, "Dove buoni uomini?" Phaethon has no doubts about his ability to recognize a good man, and when he leads Lucy to a little open terrace covered with streams and rivulets of violets and calls to her, "Courage and love," she finds herself with George. Phaethon has done all he can; the rest is up to the two English people. Once again, at least metaphorically, they are surrounded by the waters that spell meaning and salvation, and George at least is equal to the situation. His assurance and his love have grown, and he steps forward to kiss her. But before Lucy can respond she hears her name called: "the silence of life had been broken by Miss Bartlett, who stood brown against the view" (p. 86). Lucy has been brought to the brink of self-realization, of seeing air and light and love, but Charlotte's dense shadow obscures the view and helps to wither Lucy's expansiveness. There is a flash of lightning and Eager recommends courage and faith, an ironic parody of Phaethon's cry. The right values have been defeated: Lucy deceives herself, and George, whose salvation comes to depend more and more on Lucy's returning his love, is defeated too. He returns to his grayer world, his eyes drawn once more to the Why rather than to the Yes.

George's defeat and Lucy's self-deception result most of all, perhaps, from Lucy's susceptibility to the influence of others. Camped about her through most of the book is a conspiracy of people with the wrong values, the uncommitted and the aloof. These characters, although minor, are at least as interesting, and in some cases more interesting, than Lucy and George, for they are in general more complexly and more fully drawn. Lucy and George are more central than, but not so solid as, those who surround them; the two seem often, by contrast, like the prince and princess in a fairy tale; one hopes (and knows) that they will live happily ever after, but one is often more interested in the villains who seek to thwart their happiness.

The chief representatives of this group are clergymen, Mr. Eager certainly the most detestable of them. There is a marked contrast between the naturally vicious and exclusive character of the man and the pietistic phrases he mouths on all suitable occasions. His praise of "the country and its message of purity" (p. 65) is meant to contrast with his ungenerous behavior to Phaethon and Persephone, as is his speech on St. Francis with his basic lack of charity and brotherhood. It is his tendency to see life through the glass of history and art and religion, and, like Mr. Bons of "The Celestial Omnibus," he habitually takes the letter for the spirit. He is unable to see to the real heart of things, preferring as he does to impose a simplified and false order onto life's complexities. That he should love the Middle Ages and detest the Renaissance is one more sign of his damnation (as it always is in Forster's writings, where the Middle Ages represent asceticism and repression), and as the book goes on he is made to seem more and more evil. The pomposity of his speech and the rigidity of his responses to life, both of which serve to make him comic as well as evil, are the outward signs that mark him as the most unrelievedly black of all Forster's creations.

Mr. Beebe, when we first meet him, promises to give the

lie to the charge that Forster is consistently anticlerical,[2] for he is in many ways an extremely attractive person, and he is indeed meant to be a foil to Mr. Eager. But from the start his good qualities are stressed at the expense of his clerical attributes. "Mr. Beebe," Lucy remarks, "laughs just like an ordinary man" (p. 17). Mr. Beebe has not only a sense of humor, but a general affection and regard for people as well. He is able to display both tact and understanding in his personal relations, and he shows on many occasions that tolerance and sympathy lacking in the other characters of the novel. There is something, however, that keeps Mr. Beebe from being a totally admirable man. As Forster puts it, "Mr. Beebe was, from rather profound reasons, somewhat chilly in his attitude towards the other sex, and preferred to be interested rather than enthralled" (p. 44). The explanation of these profound reasons must be left until later, but it is enough to say now that in Mr. Beebe, too, there is present, however subtly, some of the medieval asceticism Forster dislikes so intensely.

The chief female villain of the novel is, of course, Charlotte Bartlett. At some earlier time in her life, Forster hints, she had been like Lucy and had had to face a situation like the one that confronts her cousin, but she had surrendered to the forces of darkness and had confused her ways of thinking and feeling. Charlotte as we now see her is the result: her reactions lack all spontaneity, following from her allegiance to this or that code of formalized behavior. Not unnaturally Charlotte contracts a friendship while in Italy with the other female goat of the book, Miss Lavish. Actually a rather pathetic maiden lady, Miss Lavish is unwilling to look squarely at the not always pleasant truth about herself and the world around her. Consequently she sets up as a lady novelist, and aesthete, a defier, according to her own lights, of convention, a romantic Bohemian luxuriating in the quaintness of Italy. She is, like Leyland in "The Story of a Panic," incapable of real appreciation of either art or nature (both of which she consistently romanticizes), for her view, wherever her eyes happen to be turned, is always closed off by her fundamental concern with herself, and her comments

2 "The Curate's Friend" does show Forster in a mood more sympathetic to clergymen.

are meant invariably not to convey information but to call attention to herself.

The one character who exemplifies the failings of all these four undesirables (and some other failings besides) is Cecil Vyse. Cecil, who falls in love with Lucy after she leaves Florence, is the most interesting and most fully explored of the minor characters. Forster comments:

> He was medieval. Like a Gothic statue. . . . He resembled those fastidious saints who guard the portals of a French cathedral. Well educated, well endowed, and not deficient physically, he remained in the grip of a certain devil whom the modern world knows as self-consciousness, and whom the medieval, with dimmer vision, worshiped as asceticism. (pp. 106–7)[3]

Cecil is the most complete representative of those qualities Forster considers medieval: he is unbending in his bearing as in his ideas; almost immediately he makes other people uncomfortable, for, although they are not always able to understand the reason for their discomfort, Cecil lacks humanity.

Cecil's reaction to Lucy reveals a good deal about him. To the reader, Lucy is most attractive for her airiness and openness, whereas to Cecil (who has clearly been reading Pater) she is most valuable for her shadow and her mystery, "like a woman of Leonardo da Vinci's, whom we love not so much for herself as for the things that she will not tell us" (p. 109). That Cecil begins immediately to regard Lucy through the dimming haze of art is characteristic, and in this he joins company with Philip Herriton and Rickie Elliot, as well as with Messrs. Eager and Beebe and Miss Lavish. Forster says that "Cecil has got something of Philip in him,"[4] and it may be said that, if Rickie is a later Philip, Cecil is an earlier one. Cecil returns from Italy feeling much as Philip did, irritable and intolerant. Unable really to enter into life, he holds it at arm's length, attempting to fix and to transform it in accordance with his view of the

---

3 It is interesting to see that here, as so often in these early novels, Forster himself makes use of artistic forms to describe his character. Cecil sees Lucy as a picture, and Forster sees Cecil as a statue. One is reminded again of the connection between Forster and those of his characters who share the aesthetic view of life.

4 Furbank and Haskell, p. 33.

"good life," a life which, in its chill immobility, lacks all the warmth and humanity of Lucy and her family.[5]

Back in England, Lucy accepts Cecil's third proposal of marriage and they are engaged. Almost immediately the Honeychurches and their neighbors begin to react to the relationship: Freddy Honeychurch puts his finger on the basic inflexibility and antiseptic quality of Cecil's mind, but it is Mr. Beebe who goes a step further and sees the essentially celibate quality of Lucy's fiancé. Cecil is, as he says, "better detached," not only from Lucy, but from the whole world, for he is unable to enter into the kind of relationship that demands equality between people. "The only relationship which Cecil conceived," Forster comments, "was feudal: that of protector and protected" (p. 189).[6] Cecil, who feels comfortable in London, not in the country, and has no profession or real interests, is the spectator par excellence, completely unable and unwilling to participate in the life around him.

That Lucy accepts Cecil's proposal at all is a sign of the confused state of her mind, but that she does not react immediately to the many distasteful traits he soon begins to exhibit reveals the depth of her confusion. Cecil dislikes intensely the happy philistinism of Windy Corner; he dislikes, too, the society of which Lucy is a part and is unable to understand her attachment to it. Lucy is bothered by Cecil but she does not know how to express her dissatisfaction. Much to Cecil's chagrin she connects him with a room without a view, but she can not pursue the implications of her feeling. She does not see that his self-conscious embrace points to his essential prudishness, that he merely cares to own her, to possess a beautiful and interesting ornament. What she does increasingly do is to compare her fiancé with the Emersons, whom she has come to see again now that they are her neighbors; somehow they are what Cecil

---

5 It should be noted that the ninth chapter, concerning Cecil's and Lucy's relationship, is entitled "Lucy as a Work of Art."

6 It is obvious that for Forster the Middle Ages, with its knights, its asceticism, and its feudal relationships, represents a life that prevents the individual from knowing himself and that artificially separates him from other people and from nature. He condemns it as he condemns those of his characters who follow the same pattern. The last chapter of the book is called "The End of the Middle Ages."

claims to be but is not. Nothing Cecil says rings true: his talk of democracy covers a more fundamental desire to be separate from people, to keep himself pure and untouched; the Emersons, on the other hand, are democratic without effort, for they love people. Lucy, of course, does not succeed fully in articulating these differences, and it is Forster who remarks: "It is obvious enough for the reader to conclude, 'She loves young Emerson.' A reader in Lucy's place would not find it obvious. . . . She loved Cecil; George made her nervous; will the reader explain to her that the phrases should have been reversed?" (pp. 174–75).

George and his father come to live near Windy Corner by chance, and George brings with him the world sorrow that has been his again since Lucy's abrupt departure from Florence after the picnic. But George finds salvation once more through a symbolic swim in a symbolic pool with Lucy's brother and Mr. Beebe. The influences of nature, of youth, of good spirits, and of camaraderie triumph, and the waters of the pool wash the grayness from his soul, confirming his resolution to win Lucy's love. His fight is a difficult one, for by now Lucy's defenses against the truth are stronger than they were in Italy, but he is helped by the comparisons Lucy continues to make between him and Cecil. She perceives in George, above all, a strenuous effort to do whatever he is engaged in as well as he can, and naturally Cecil seems less attractive than ever by comparison. His stiff attempts at Meredithian comedy come off badly beside George's unpremeditated enthusiasms; Cecil's place, it becomes increasingly apparent, is not on the field, but along the sidelines of life.

But Lucy's growing if partly unconscious regard for George is checked by an unexpected incident. George and Lucy hear Cecil read a description from a second-rate novel of what turns out to be their first kiss (the pseudonymous author is Miss Lavish), and as Lucy goes off to cover her embarrassment, George follows her and kisses her again. George, as usual, tries to bring Lucy back from art to life, but once more Lucy lies to herself and the pretended wins out over the real. She orders George to leave the house forever, despite his protestations of love, and he goes, as he says, back into the darkness again. But Lucy is not totally unaffected: though she refuses his love, his words remain with her and almost immediately she is able to see how selfish and pompous her fiancé is. She is finally capable of recognizing the truth about others, if not about herself (or George, for if she were able to see him truly, she would be forced to learn something about herself), and that night she breaks her engagement to Cecil.

The scene between Lucy and Cecil is handled with great subtlety and understanding. To Cecil, Lucy seems more and more desirable now that he is about to lose her. "He looked at her, instead of through her, for the first time since they were engaged. From a Leonardo she had become a living woman, with mysteries and forces of her own, with qualities that even eluded art" (p. 210). The role into which he is cast calls forth whatever is best in him, and he is able, for the moment, to be noble, unselfish, and free from affectation. Lucy, on the other hand, is guilty as well as confused. Deep within her, unacknowledged but active, lies her love for George, and her desire to hide it both from herself and from Cecil makes her more brutal than she usually is. Primed for an argument, she becomes increasingly furious with Cecil's dignified responses, and it is he who this once wins our admiration. "On the landing he paused, strong in his renunciation, and gave her a look of memorable beauty. For all his culture, Cecil was an ascetic at heart, and nothing in his love became him like the leaving of it" (p. 213).

Lucy continues to lie to herself, and she soon makes concrete her intention to run from love and truth by arranging, with the help of Charlotte and Mr. Beebe, a trip to Greece with two old ladies. As the time for her departure approaches, Lucy becomes more and more disagreeable and sensitive to criticism. Her mother tells her that she is coming to resemble Charlotte, and she is, for she has ceased to act in accordance with either her head or her heart. In a way she recalls Rickie Elliot, since, like him, she has lost her ability to perceive reality and has allowed herself to adopt dishonest values. Given Lucy's lack of self-awareness and her lack of a sense of tragedy in life, however, one sees her, if one is to imagine her persisting in self-deception, not dying young like Rickie, but growing old like Charlotte. What saves her from that fate is the fact that she is susceptible to good as well as to bad influences, and the last act of Lucy's drama is played out in the presence of the notably good character, Mr. Emerson.

Mr. Emerson is, as E. K. Brown called him, the chief "redemptive character" [7] of the book. In him are embodied all the values of the novel that Forster considers worthwhile, as all the bad ones are in Cecil. He possesses an almost boundless capacity for love, and the Charlottes and Cecils of the novel, who are themselves incapable of love,[8] are unable to understand him. But however bad Mr. Emerson's relations are with Cecil or Charlotte, they are worse still with Mr. Eager, for Mr. Emerson represents true religious feeling. Listening to Mr. Eager's lecture in Santa Croce ("built by faith in the full fervour of medievalism") on Giotto's fresco of the Ascension of St. John ("untroubled by the snares of anatomy and perspective" [p. 33]), Mr. Emerson spontaneously bursts out: "No! . . . Remember nothing of the sort. Built by faith indeed! That simply means the workmen weren't paid properly. And as for the frescoes, I see no truth in them. Look at that fat man in blue! He must weigh as much as I do, and he is shooting into the sky like an air-balloon" (p. 33). It is true that there is at times something childishly straightforward about Mr. Emerson's responses to things around him, but it is also true that his responses to people are always right, born as they are of genuine affection and respect. Furthermore, Mr. Emerson's reactions are at times exaggerated so that they may contrast with those of the Eagers of the book. Mr. Emerson, who more than any other character in the novel sees life directly, refuses to accept even the conventions of art (as in his reaction to St. John, the "fat man in blue"), refuses to view anything at any time aesthetically. If this directness of his makes him somewhat naïve in the realm of art, it makes him also a much more admirable person than Mr. Eager and Cecil, who view all life at a distance.

7 E. K. Brown, "The Revival of E. M. Forster," *Forms of Modern Fiction*, ed. by William Van O'Connor (Minneapolis: The University of Minnesota Press, 1948), p. 165.

8 In an interview with Angus Wilson, Forster said, in answer to one of Wilson's questions about the sheep and the goats in his novels: "The goats are. . . . Well, failure to love marks them." See "A Conversation with E. M. Forster," *Encounter*, IX (November, 1957), p. 53.

From the beginning Lucy conceives an affection for the old man, an affection that increases in proportion to Cecil's contempt for him. Now, as she is about to depart for Greece, she meets Mr. Emerson—accidentally, as it appears—and is forced into a conversation with him. Lucy is disconcerted at the meeting, for it is more difficult for her, even unconsciously, to lie to Mr. Emerson than to her mother, to Cecil, or to herself. Truth and love are too much a part of Mr. Emerson for her to be able to confront him boldly with falsehood. Lucy's confusion and muddle become more and more apparent, and it suddenly flashes upon the old man that Lucy loves his son. Lucy tries to appear shocked and disgusted, but Mr. Emerson delivers to her what is probably the central speech of the book:

"I only wish poets would say this, too: that love is of the body; not the body, but of the body. Ah! the misery that would be saved if we confessed that! *Ah for a little directness to liberate the soul!* Your soul, dear Lucy! I hate the word now, because of all the cant with which superstition has wrapped it round. But we have souls. I cannot say how they came nor whither they go, but we have them, and I see you ruining yours. I cannot bear it. It is again the darkness creeping in; it is hell." Then he checked himself. "What nonsense I have talked—how abstract and remote! And I have made you cry! Dear girl, forgive my prosiness; marry my boy. When I think what life is, and how seldom love is answered by love—Marry him; it is one of the moments for which the world is made." (pp. 247–48)[9]

Love, passion, honesty; directness and the soul: Lucy does not completely understand, but somehow she does begin to see to the bottom of her own soul. She is frightened, but she is saved; clear-minded, honest with herself once more, she is again ready to love and to live as a whole and integral individual.

In the last chapter of the book Lucy and George, now

9 Italics mine. The point of having Mr. Emerson react precisely as he does to the picture of St. John, to the corpulence of the "man in blue," becomes even clearer after this speech. The *body* draws his attention, the physical and tangible reality of human presence, stripped of its artistic cloak. The human form may assume many shapes in art as in life, but it is, in Mr. Emerson's opinion, confusing and wrong to assume that it can fly, that its heft or limitations can be ignored. Although love is not entirely a physical phenomenon, it must contain the physical: it is "of the body," grounded in the reality that, for Mr. Emerson, will have nothing to do with the artificial or the factitious.

married, are back at the Pension Bertolini. It is some six months after Lucy's talk with Mr. Emerson, and the ending of the fairy tale is at hand. Unlike fairy tales, however, the novel leaves the reader with an awareness not only of good triumphant, but of bad still active in the world outside: although the villains have been worsted, they have not completely left the scene. The Honeychurches, it seems, have not forgiven Lucy and George, and it is Mr. Beebe who appears to be responsible for their attitude. It is the clergyman who, of all the characters in the novel, reacts most unfavorably to the news that Lucy loves George. His attitude, if unexpected, is explainable, for throughout the novel there are indications that beneath, and more fundamental than, his tolerance and humor, there is the asceticism Forster connects with the clerical mind. "Mr. Emerson was profoundly religious," Forster comments, "and differed from Mr. Beebe chiefly by his acknowledgment of passion" (p. 244). It is the lack of real passion in the clergyman that finally tells against his character, for it affects his attitude not only to sex but to life in general. Mr. Beebe can never face life as fully and strenuously as George Emerson; between him and it there rises the fiction of knight-errantry, a fiction that appears to him more real than the real love of George and Lucy.

The fact that Mr. Beebe proves at the last to belong with the Cecils and the Eagers and that his influence works against Lucy's and George's complete happiness says something about the book as a whole: the aesthetic view of life has suffered a setback but has not been obliterated; it is still a potential, if not a very active, threat. Although *A Room with a View* is the last of Forster's novels in which the fight against that vision is the central problem, the problem does not disappear from his later books. *A Room with a View* is, in a way, a watershed between Forster's first two and his last two novels: its happy ending, its triumphant love affair, and its rejection of Cecil and his kind mark the victorious conclusion of the battle that is the subject of the first three books—the battle in which the armies of the active and the participating vanquish the benighted armies of the spectators.

At the same time the book prepares indirectly for the central theme of the last two novels, the search for order. That search is, of course, not absent from the earlier books, but it becomes more active now that its chief enemy is in retreat. In *A Room with a View* the search for order is largely George's, and the last chapter shows its results. Lucy, who throughout the novel fails to interest the reader as much as she might because of her lack of self-awareness, becomes a more substantial figure: "When it came to the point, it was she who remembered the past, she into whose soul the iron had entered" (p. 252). George, however, disappoints: "He was a boy, after all" (p. 252); "his own content was absolute, but hers held bitterness" (p. 253). George has found his love, and his searches are over. What is troublesome is not that George has found his solution in personal relations and love, but that he no longer seems aware of the question mark with which he began. One must affirm the transitory Yes, says Mr. Emerson, but George's road has led from the transitory No, through the Center of Indifference, to the *everlasting* Yes. He no longer realizes that the Yes is transitory; his search for meaning has come to an abrupt halt. Somehow one does not feel that the problems George himself raises are adequately answered by his love for Lucy; too much is wrong with the world, too much remains unsolved. The twelve winds that blow us hither for no known reason and then blow us away again are not to be forgotten so easily. George, rather abruptly for one who suffers and thinks so much, loses awareness of his earlier doubts, and he is a lesser, if a happier, person as a result. As Stephan Wonham failed to answer the issues posed by Rickie Elliot, so George fails to meet his own. Once again Forster has lost his balance in his exaltation of the physical, the instinctive, the vital. Only George's quest, not his discovery, is of the intellect, and the reader, although he shares George's happiness, is also conscious of waste, of promise unfulfilled.

It is Forster himself who continues George's search, puts the question mark back into life, notes the transitoriness of the Yes, for his next two novels presuppose the questions that George does not answer. *A Room with a View* is a holiday for Forster; as Lucy, sitting at her piano in an early scene of the novel and reflecting that Beethoven's sonatas "can triumph or despair as the player decides," makes up her mind that she will "play on the side of victory" (p. 40), that Beethoven's sonatas will triumph, so Forster makes his novel triumph. The problems of everyday life are not gone, but they are either conquered or, temporarily and almost successfully, suppressed. Holidays have always in them an element of regret, an awareness that they exist, as it were, out of time. *A Room with a View* is no exception, and in its happiness there exist the seeds of future discontent, portents of a less perfect future.[10]

10 An article by Forster, marking the fiftieth anniversary of the book's publication, "A View without a Room," *The Observor*, No. 8717 (July 27, 1958), 15, traces the subsequent careers of the book's leading characters and provides an interesting footnote to the novel.

3 · Two Worlds and Their Ways: The Short Stories

FORSTER PUBLISHED his first short story in 1903, his last in 1920, so that the dates of publication of the tales are roughly parallel to those of the novels: about one-third of them appeared in the two years prior to the appearance of *Where Angels Fear to Tread*, and the last was published four years before *A Passage to India*.[1] The stories are less ambitious than the novels, but it is their conceptions rather than their length that makes most of them minor works of art. The shorter works are more overtly

---

1 According to Forster, the stories were all written before the First World War. The dates of their publication are as follows (* indicates that the story appeared in *The Celestial Omnibus*, † that it appeared in *The Eternal Moment*):

    1903 "Albergo Empedocle," *Temple Bar*
    1904 "The Story of a Panic," *The Independent Review* *
           "The Road from Colonus," *The Independent Review* *
           "The Other Side of the Hedge," *The Independent Review* *
    1905 "The Eternal Moment," *The Independent Review* †
    1907 "The Curate's Friend," *Putnam's Magazine* *
    1908 "The Celestial Omnibus," *The Albany Review* *
    1909 "Other Kingdom," *The English Review* *
           "The Machine Stops," *The Oxford and Cambridge Review* †
    1911 "The Point of It," *The English Review* †
           "Mr. Andrews," *The Open Window* †
    1912 "Cooperation," *The English Review* †
    1920 "The Story of the Siren," *The Hogarth Press*.†

The name of "Cooperation" was later changed to "Co-ordination." "The Story of the Siren" was published as a separate pamphlet. "The Story of a Panic" was, according to Forster, the first written of his tales. K. W. Grandsen, in his *E. M. Forster* (p. 11), refers to an unpublished story, "The Rock."

fabulous and moral, even tendentious, based as they are on a pointed opposition between the forces of good and the forces of evil, an opposition unrelieved by the more subtle investigations into the psychological complexities of the leading characters that one finds in the novels. However, if the too manifest intentions of the stories limit their artistic value, they only enhance their usefulness as guides to Forster's preoccupations and to the changes in mood and direction of his work in his most creative years.

The stories were gathered, in 1911 and in 1928, into two collections, and Forster seems to have aimed at creating in each a distinct unity of tone and mood. Certainly he chose to omit from *The Celestial Omnibus* of 1911 several tales which had already been published and which were later included in *The Eternal Moment*, with whose spirit they have much more in common. The difference between the two volumes can be most clearly illustrated by referring to some of Forster's statements at the time. In the year that his first story appeared, there also was founded a new magazine, *The Independent Review*. Forster wrote many years later:

Can you imagine decency touched with poetry? It was thus that the 'Independent' appeared to us—a light rather than a fire, but a light that penetrated the emotions. . . . The first number lies of the table as I write: as fresh and attractive to hold as when I bought it on a book stall at St Pancras thirty years back, and thought the new age had begun. (*GLD*, p. 116)

In the next two years four of Forster's stories were published in its pages, and when *The Celestial Omnibus* was issued, it was dedicated "To the Memory of the Independent Review." The exuberance and enthusiasm that Forster felt for "the new age" is reflected in this volume, as it is in the early, particularly the so-called Italian, novels, and together these two bodies of work help to define Forster's thought and attitudes during the early years of the century.

In 1920, when Forster published the last of his stories, he wrote a short essay called "Happiness!" wherein he told how "in the heart of each man there is contrived, by desperate devices a magical island. . . . We place it in the past or the future for safety, for we dare not locate it in the present. . . . We call it a memory or a vision to lend it solidity, but it is neither really; it is the outcome of our sadness, and of our disgust with the world that we have made" (AH, p. 49). The tales that Forster brought together for *The Eternal Moment* are, on the whole, more somber in tone than those in the first volume, closer in spirit to the last two than to the first three novels. There is less merriment, less hope, less in the way of a realizable ideal. The distinction is not absolute; Forster's progress through his stories, as through his novels, involves anticipatory leaps as well as retrospective glances. While the same problems often recur, however, the gradual darkening of the landscape in which they are introduced is apparent, and it seems fair enough to regard the anticipation of a new age and the vision of a magical island as the symbolic termini of his career.

If Forster felt in 1903 that he was at the beginning of a better time, he was not so sanguine as to imagine that all was well in his world. The early stories are confident but not complacent: confident that evil can be recognized and overcome— or, at any rate, escaped. What marks the work in *The Celestial Omnibus* is an assurance of tone that derives from the lightly satirical technique and from the author's sense of complicity with his audience. It is always clear, to the reader if not to the characters, where right lies, and he is invited, very much as he is in *A Room with a View*, to laugh whenever the transparent villain enters the scene. The recurrent pattern, to which almost all of the stories conform, introduces a group of bogusly sophisticated prigs, pedants, and pompous businessmen who do their best to suppress the imaginative vitality and natural feeling of Forster's heroes. The characteristic images of the stories are fences and gates, locks and keys, and to the protagonists society is a prison from which they attempt to break free. Generally they succeed and find a new home in what, in one of the stories, is called "Other Kingdom," a kingdom whose virtues are compounded of ninteenth-century Wordsworthianism and Hellenism and, more generally, derive from the whole primitivistic tradition of the last two hundred years. Like Matthew Arnold, Forster sought some release from "this iron time/Of doubts, disputes, distractions, fears," and found it in nature, children, myth, in all that suggested, as Arnold said in the same poem, "The freshness of the early world."

Several of the early stories illustrate almost too clearly the struggle between "this iron time" and "the early world." In "The Celestial Omnibus," for example, the conflict is symbolized by the opposing figures of the small boy, whose ingenuousness wins him an enthusiastic reception in the ideal heaven of the story, and the snobbish Mr. Bons, who owns seven editions of Shelley and a vellum-bound set of Dante and who announces unctuously to the boy that he has "never doubted the essential truth of Poetry" (p. 65). The difference between them is cleverly revealed in the opening lines—"The boy who resided at Agathox Lodge, 28, Buckingham Park Road, Surbiton . . ." (p. 49)—where the simple reference to the nameless boy is qualified by the pedantically precise indication of his address. The address, in fact, is his parents', and they, along with Mr. Bons, belong to the world of the letter, with its numbers, measurements, and limitations, whereas their son's kingdom is of the spirit. "Tickets on this line," Sir Thomas Browne tells the boy as he is driving him to heaven, ". . . can be purchased by coinage from no terrene mint. And a chronometer . . . can acquire by no mutation the double-cake that charms the fangless Cerberus of heaven!" (p. 57).

It is not surprising, therefore, that when the boy returns from his first trip to the timeless, unconfined realm of the creative spirit to tell his parents of his discovery, he is caned, locked into his room, and made to memorize a poem as a punishment. The story contrives its largest effects through irony, and the irony reaches its climax as the boy recites to Mr. Bons Keats's sonnet, "Standing aloof in giant ignorance." "So for a few moments," Forster comments, "the wise man and the ignorant boy were left alone in the smoking-room" (p. 64). The omnibus, as Sir Thomas remarks, "Omnibus est" (p. 56): it is for all, and so the next day Mr. Bons, who has come with the boy in order to disprove his story, finds himself, to his horror, in a coach being driven by Dante. It is the poet who delivers the story's moral, when he tells the terrified Bons, who can see none of the beautiful things the boy points out to him: "I am the means and not the end. I am the food and not the life. . . .

For poetry is a spirit; and they that would worship it must worship in spirit and in truth" (p. 73). This Bons cannot do, and as he crawls from the omnibus he falls and vanishes, shrieking that he sees London, where the next day his mangled body is discovered.

But the boy remains; freed forever from the uncomprehending and rigid adults, he enters into Forster's uninhibitedly eclectic heaven, joining Keats and Shelley, Mrs. Gamp and Achilles, Wagner and Dickens, and all those whose lives refuse the limiting categories of time and space. Writers and their creations mingle here with musicians and their music, and the whole world of the creative imagination is open to whoever can enter it as a child. This the boy does, and though the world of Surbiton remains what it has always been—a replica of the stuffy, overly ordered society of Sawston in Forster's first two novels—still a claim has been made for the ideal, for that reality behind the appearances to which the Rhinemaidens refer when they sing to the boy of "Truth in the depth, truth on the height" (p. 62).

The protagonist of "The Other Side of the Hedge" discovers the truth of Sir Thomas Browne's observation on chronometers when he crosses from his side of the hedge, where he has all his life been walking along a dusty and monotonous road, to the other side, where he sees blue sky, green grass, and a landscape "that one might have called . . . a park, or garden, if the words did not imply a certain triviality and constraint" (p. 41). There his pedometer, which has heretofore marked his progress through the years, refuses to work. He has entered, by way of a pool whose waters symbolize (as in so much of Forster's work) baptism and regeneration, into what Dickens called "tother world," a place which, one of the characters in the tale remarks, "means nothing but itself" (p. 44). Forster's other world is less frightening than Dickens'; represented in most of his fiction by nature and suggesting tradition, continuity, and human habitation, it is as far from the savage landscapes of D. H. Lawrence as from the civilized cities of the English who live in Sawston and Surbiton. At its wildest, nature is for Forster still European, a part of the Mediterranean harmony he was later to set forth as an ideal in A Passage to India. But like

Dickens', Forster's otherness is unlimited by the three dimensions and the hard circumstantiality of the normal world. Here, where there is "beauty and extent" (p. 42) and movement, but neither time nor development, "a man of fifty or sixty" has the "voice . . . of a boy of eighteen" (p. 41).

Like the heaven of "The Celestial Omnibus," the other side of the hedge is Forster's vision of perfect being, but the protagonist of the story is benighted enough to think that he is in a prison. In fact, it is from prison that he has emerged, in leaving behind the specious pursuit of scientific knowledge and progress, but this he does not realize until he has been led by his companion from the first to the second of the places where the two sides of the hedge are joined. Forster's allegory is based upon a reference to the mythological gates of ivory and horn, through which pass, respectively, false dreams and true. The first of the gates opens outwards onto the brown road, and "it is through this gate," we are told, "that humanity went out countless ages ago, when it was first seized with the desire to walk" (p. 45). The gate of horn opens inwards, and here at last the protagonist surrenders his fierce desire for "life, with its struggles and victories, with its failures and hatreds, with its deep moral meaning and its unknown goal!" (p. 47). The effort to become gives way to the willingness to be, as the hero sinks into a sleep which, again in Dickensian fashion, indicates the passage from one state to another. "This is where your road ends," his companion tells him, "and through this gate humanity—all that is left of it—will come in to us" (p. 48).

"The Other Side of the Hedge" is a clever story, but it is too badly allegorical in its attack on modern society. A better use of mythology for these purposes is made in "Other Kingdom," a rendering of the Ovidian story of Daphne and Apollo in a modern English setting. The geography of the story recalls the contrasting sides of the hedge: a small stream flows between the domain of Harcourt Worters, an egocentric and possessive businessman, and Other Kingdom Copse, a small beech wood where, as the Latin lesson which opens the story indicates, the gods have lived (*habitarunt di quoque silvas*). Like Cecil Vyse, Harcourt has no view, but he has a good deal of money—he is Midas as well as Apollo in the story—and a profound attachment to the things of this world. Among these he numbers Evelyn Beaumont, whom he has brought from primitive Ireland to civilized England in order to develop her soul and marry her.

If Harcourt's principal desire is to own, Evelyn's is to be free, and gradually the inevitable conflict develops between them, with Other Kingdom as the battleground. The beech copse is Worters' gift to his fiancée, and her ecstatic reaction is a sign not that possession has turned her head, as the toadying narrator of the tale conjectures, but that she is in sympathy with the spirit of the woods. From the beginning she is like a tree herself, full of quivering lights and shades, her green dress an emblem of her elemental and unspoiled nature. Her disappointment at discovering that she is to have the woods on a ninety-nine year lease has the same source as her remark about the naiad, who "has had a headache for nineteen hundred years" (p. 86). Instinctively she yearns for what is open, light, and unconfined, and these qualities she finds, like Forster, in the symbols of the pre-Christian world. (The stories might have as their motto Swinburne's apostrophe to Christ: "The world has grown grey with thy breath.") Harcourt's world is preeminently modern and gray, and though he does eventually make Evelyn a present of the woods for ever, he makes it clear that Other Kingdom is to become part of the earthbound Worters estate. He will put up, he says, "a simple fence . . . just like what I have put round my garden and the fields. Then at the other side of the copse, away from the house, I would put a gate, and have keys—two keys, I think—one for me and one for you— not more" (p. 94).

Keys, gates, fences, locks: Worters is the archetypal jailer of the early tales, and Evelyn is increasingly frightened to feel herself being closed in. "I must be on the outside," she cries, "I must be where anyone can reach me" (p. 96). Harcourt's behavior causes her to languish. She gives up green dresses for brown; the winter of the spirit settles over her. There is no way out of the impasse—not in a society dominated by Worters at any rate—and Forster, following Ovid, resorts to metamorphosis for an answer. Evelyn, fulfilling the wish expressed by the heroine of an old song for "the wings of an Angel" to fly "o'er these prison walls," grows just such wings, becomes a pagan angel, a dryad. Leaving behind her fiancé and his family, she disappears into the beech woods. "She danced away," the narrator remembers, "from our society and our life, back, back, through the centuries till houses and fences fell and the earth lay wild to the sun" (p. 108).

Other Kingdom, then, like the heaven of "The Celestial Omnibus" or the land on the other side of the hedge, is a dreamlike projection of certain qualities absent from contemporary society. Between the modern and the better there runs, in each of the stories, a river or stream which only a few can cross. And it is worthwhile observing the sad fact that, if men like Worters and Bons are excluded from participation in the kingdom of the ideal, Evelyn and the boy are equally unable to return to what is, however disappointingly, the home of the real. That point is made in "Albergo Empedocle," the first tale Forster published and the only one he chose not to include in either of his collections. At the end of that story the hero, Harold, has been declared mad, and, unable any longer to speak English, he is put away in an asylum. The story takes place in Sicily at the Empedocles Inn, so that the ancient Greek world is its spiritual setting. Empedocles, because of his belief in the transmigration of souls, serves as the symbol of what happens to Harold: the embodiment of imagination, vitality, and uncorrupted feeling, he returns through the centuries to a Greece that is conceived as the home of athletic, handsome, spontaneous, healthily sensuous men.

Harold's retreat from his own century is caused by the frustration of his power to love and his desire for truth (in *Where Angels Fear to Tread*, Philip must learn "human love and love of truth"), and both are thwarted by his fiancée, Mildred. Traveling through Europe with Mildred and her family, Harold is entirely content with everything life offers him; it is generally acknowledged by the Peaslakes that Harold is the physical, whereas Mildred is the intellectual, center of the party. But it is to Harold that there comes the sensation of having lived in Acragas before. He only knows, he tells the excited Mildred, who is a great devotee of the imagination, that he was greater, that he was better, saw better, heard better, thought better, and loved better. To Harold the important

thing is that Mildred believes him; to her it is the chance to
turn their love into a classical idyll, and she immediately begins
to induce in herself the belief that she has lived in Acragas with
Harold. When he quietly tells her that she has not, he unwittingly brings their relation to an end. Mildred, afraid, angry,
and mortified, refuses any longer to believe him, and when
Harold discovers her disbelief, he calmly announces: "This is
the end." By the next morning he is apparently back in his
earlier state. "But I firmly believe that he has been a Greek,"
his friend, the narrator, writes at the end of the story, "nay,
that he is a Greek. . . . For the greater has replaced the less,
and he is living the life he knew to be greater than the life he
lived with us. And I also believe, that if things had happened
otherwise, he might be living that greater life among us." [2]

Harold is the greater, but the greater, it seem, inevitably
suffers humiliation in modern society. In one sense the story
records the triumph of the ideal, but in another its defeat. Confronted by ancient Greece, society locks it in a madhouse and
announces that it cannot communicate with it. The greater has
replaced the less, but the less continues to rule the world. "Albergo Empedocle" makes clear what is implicit in the other
stories we have read, namely, that in a world composed of what
Gide called "crustaceans," there is no place for the love and
truth Forster's heroes and heroines cherish. However much the
stories intend and in fact manage to expose the inveterate
secondhandedness of the spectators and manipulators of life,
however determinedly they mean to give the palm to those who
are open and expansive, still their endings tell a different tale.
All of these stories conclude with the presumptive victors off
in the woods or up in heaven, showing, disappointingly, more
discretion than valor. One is only sure that they have run away,
but not, as the proverb promises, that they will fight again
another day.

Is it just to be so literalist about fantasy or to demand that
fantasy win all the battles it fights? The answer to the second
question is obviously no, or would be, if the stories themselves
did not suggest that a victory had been won, if there were not a

discrepancy between the moods and the facts of the tales. The first question is harder. According to Forster, fantasy asks us to "pay something extra" (*AN*, p. 103), asks us to enter a world with its own laws, its own logic, its own codes of behavior. But Forster's fantasies, unlike those of Max Beerbohm or David Garnett, are "impure": they are not simply tales, but moral tales, and they demand of the reader, therefore, not only that he surrender his belief so far as to accept dryads or a magical omnibus, but also that he make comparisons at the same time between the ideal realm of which they are part and the more prosaic, "normal" world. "I am not well satisfied with them," Goldsworthy Lowes Dickinson wrote in a famous criticism of the short stories. "Your constant pre-occupation to bring realistic life into contact with the background of values (or whatever it is) is very difficult to bring off, and I am apt to feel the cleft" (*GLD*, p. 216). The trouble with these tales, to pursue Dickinson's line, is that their parts fail to cohere, and Forster's contention that "the power of fantasy penetrates into every corner of the universe" (*AN*, p. 104) is rarely illustrated in his own work, where fantasy is likely to have a corner all to itself.

The important point is that Forster is after two different things in the tales: he aims to demolish through satire and to rebuild through fantasy. The destructive criticism is solid and sure; the element of fantasy remains elusive and not completely convincing. In *The Longest Journey*, Rickie says of one of his colleagues:

He cheers one up. He does believe in poetry. Smart, sentimental books do seem absolutely absurd to him, and gods and fairies far nearer to reality. He tries to express all modern life in the terms of Greek mythology, because the Greeks looked very straight at things, and Demeter and Aphrodite are thinner veils than "The survival of the fittest," or "A marriage has been arranged," and other draperies of modern journalese.

When Agnes asks him if he knows what that means, he answers: "It means that poetry, not prose, lies at the core" (pp. 196–97). One is tempted to repeat Agnes' question and to ask it equally of Other Kingdom, the other side of the hedge, and the heaven of "The Celestial Omnibus." It is possible to say something of each of these symbols, to put into general terms the nature of the ideal, but conceptually as well as artistically these symbols are inadequate vehicles of the meanings they are meant to bear. Harold may serve as an example. All the primitivism of "Albergo Empedocle" is represented by him. It is he whose mind is freed from logic in the dream world that leads him back to ancient Acragas, he who catches up in himself all that was vital in the ancient Greek world, all that is lost to modern society. But the reader, not swept away from the critical vantage point that Forster himself has established, is apt to be critical of Harold and of the Greek ideal in the form it is here presented as being too mindless and exclusively athletic to function as significant counterweights to the evils of the twentieth century.

Harold is a preliminary sketch for Stephen Wonham in *The Longest Journey*, and his good qualities, like Stephen's, have to be accepted by the reader as a matter of faith. Inevitably so, since Forster, in attempting to articulate in his characters an ideal state of being, works largely through negatives. His heroes do not do anything, they do not think anything, and they rarely say anything. Activity, except when, like swimming or running, it is done for its own sake, is the mark of businessmen like Harcourt Worters or educationists like Miss Eliza Dimbleby, who passes the protagonist of "The Other Side of the Hedge" while he is still pursuing his unknown goal. The intellectuals of the tales are the pedant Bons and the snob Mildred Peaslake, and talk, to quote a character in one of Joyce Cary's novels, "is lies." Interestingly, it is through conversation that Forster achieves his best effects in the stories. The objectionable characters are constantly revealing in various remarks their pettiness, their insincerity, and their obtuseness, and they are for that reason amusing and alive. The heroes, on the other hand, neither change nor talk nor work. They cannot be satirized because they are too good, they cannot be analyzed because they are too simple, and so they suffer the fate of many good characters in fiction: they are unbelievable and they are dull. On the whole, Forster does better with his ideal when he presents it through landscape. The trees, the rivers, and the hills come alive in a way that Evelyn and the boy never do, and they are therefore the more convincing as symbols of the other world as well.

In only one of these four tales is there a hero—and his part is minor—of the kind who, if developed, might pull together the disparate elements of the tales and make them into organic wholes. This is Ford, of whom the narrator of "Other Kingdom" says that he "has dreams . . . but dreams of the tangible and the actual: robust dreams, which take him, not to heaven, but to another earth" (pp. 83–84). Ford is a student of the classics. It is he, Evelyn comes to realize, whom she loves, and he is the only one who understands her. Ford, too, is capable of approaching the ideal, and although the road he chooses to reach it is not as spectacular as Evelyn's, it is an honest and, presumably, a successful one. When last seen, he is reading his Sophocles, and he is, to every reader's satisfaction, given the last word against his guardian, the irate Worters. In this story at least, the forces of light come off not too badly in this, as well as in Other Kingdom.

They come off still better in "The Curate's Friend," a sketchy but suggestive story, in the form of an anecdote, relating the conversion of a clergyman, neither from nor to religion, but from one way of thinking and feeling to another. Jocose and conventional to begin with, the curate mysteriously meets— or, rather, is chosen as a companion by—a faun who, as the symbol of truth and spontaneity, forces him to recognize his self-consciousness and insincerity. Once he has accepted the faun as a friend, he becomes a different man: he learns that nature is alive, he can hear the chalk downs singing to each other at night, and he ceases to talk of self-denial and Satan. But he makes no dramatic escapes from the world of everyday as a beech tree or an ancient Greek. He goes on, and even advances materially, in the religious life, and although his chief desires are to do good, to communicate his joy, and to help others, he is, in no bad sense, worldly and realistic.

"The Curate's Friend," then, is something of an anomaly among the stories we have looked at, and it differs from them not only in its theme and its resolution but in its characterization as well. The clergyman, conceived as one who will remain in his parish at the end rather than escaping to a fantasy land, is more complex than any of the other protagonists. Though drawn to a smaller scale, he comes much closer to the characters in the early novels, and it is significant that the single dramatic incident in his story, the one that leads up to his conversion, is a recurrent, almost an obsessive one in those books. To win the clergyman's friendship and trust, the faun agrees to make his fiancée happy. This he does by pushing her into the arms of another man, with whom she is harmlessly flirting, and there follows an embrace and a declaration of love. The curate is a witness to the scene, and like Philip watching Caroline and Gino, like Rickie secretly observing Agnes and Gerald, like Charlotte coming upon Lucy and George, he reacts strongly to what he sees. But his reaction is curious; like the others, he is essentially an outsider, looking on from a distance that is both physical and psychological, and although he berates the faun, he is not really unhappy. "Does he cry?" asks the faun, and the hill answers: "His eyes are as dry as pebbles" (p. 122). As he comes, with the faun's urging, to acknowledge the truth of his own feelings, and as he begins to experience the joy that remains with him in the years that follow, it becomes clear that he has learned something important about himself: that, like Cecil Vyse, he is "better detached."

It is tempting to think of the faun as a projection of the curate's most fundamental desires and to treat his discovery not as one of being (as it is, say, in "The Other Side of the Hedge") but of his own being, as a psychological rather than a metaphysical truth. Like Philip Herriton, he has been saved from marriage, saved from sexual experience, and though he continues to live the life of this world, it is as a clergyman who can "look down upon" (p. 123) the members of his congregation. Speaking of his experience, he says: "I can tell no one exactly how it came to me. For if I breathed one word of that, my present life, so agreeable and profitable, would come to an end, my congregation would depart, and so should I, and instead of being an asset to my parish, I might find myself an expense to the nation" (p. 124). It is easy enough to read the curate's speech in the light of the other stories, to see in the prison or madhouse to which the final words refer society's habitual weapon against those who cherish the ideal. If, though, the story operates on a psychological level as well, it may be necessary to find other reasons for the curate's secrecy and fear and other explanations for society's potential disapproval. One comes back to the curate's fiancée, to his broken engagement, to his joy in his release, to his subsequent life with his friend the faun, "sitting before the beech copse as a man sits before his house" (p. 123). If it is too extreme to suggest that in the curate's response to his fiancée and to the faun there is implied some covertly homosexual element, it can in any case be said that his attitudes are in defiance of normative behavior, and that if the curate has not done what society condemns, he has at least failed to do what society expects of him—or would expect, if it knew, for, as he says, he has "been forced to use the unworthy medium of a narrative, and to delude you by declaring that this is a short story, suitable for reading in the train" (p. 124).

Whether one chooses to regard "The Curate's Friend" as an account of a man's awakening to the knowledge and acceptance of his most secret desires or, more directly, as a celebration of a successful personal relation, however bizarre and disguised, it remains true that the story is an unusual one in the Forster canon. Forster's heroes and heroines are rarely happy (at least if they remain within the confines of society), still more rarely happy in their attachments (George and Lucy are the exception). In the five stories we have looked at there are three unsuccessful engagements and no marriages. *Where Angels Fear to Tread* is a tangle of frustrations; and in *The Longest Journey* there is, among many unhappy marriages, only one, Stephen's, that succeeds, and that one is difficult to credit. It has often been remarked that Forster is more successful at praising than at presenting personal relations; Rickie's sentimental and quasi-sexual feeling for Stephen and Philip's for Gino are in many ways the closest approximation to passion in the books, and both are, in social terms, incapable of fulfillment. The failure of human beings to contact one another is one of Forster's leading themes, and it is very likely the chief cause of the pervasive sense of frustration in his work. Stories like "Other Kingdom" raise the problem and then, in their endings, manage to evade it; "The Curate's Friend" and *A Room with a View* are the rare cases where the protagonists are able to get the best of both worlds; and the most interesting of Forster's writings, like the two remaining stories in *The Celestial Omnibus*, are those which acknowledge the difficult relation between desire and fulfillment and make drama out of the struggle.

"The Story of a Panic" is, in its main outlines, a tale very much like "The Celestial Omnibus" or "Other Kingdom." Its two principal events are an epiphany, in which the god Pan reveals himself to a group of English picnickers in the woods above Ravello, and the aftermath of that revelation, in which Eustace Robinson, Forster's fourteen-year-old hero, is locked into a small room with bars on the window. Pan's appearance is an ironic commentary on the attitudes and beliefs of most of the people at the outing, a characteristic assortment of Forsterian villains: Leyland, the pseudoartist, who complains that nature's "colouring is monotonous and crude" (p. 6); Sandbach, the minister and Eustace's tutor, who sonorously announces that the great god Pan is dead; and Tytler, the philistine narrator of the tale, who takes Eustace's perpetual lounging and loafing as almost a personal affront. But they are all wrong, and particularly Tytler, for Eustace's refusal to do anything is a sign of grace, and it is therefore to him that the god reveals himself in his benign and life-giving form. Fitting the visitation to the capacities of those who are visited, Forster plays on the two meanings of the god's name: to the adult members of the party he comes as terror (the panic of the story's title), while to Eustace he is the revelation of "all" (Pan), of the power and beauty of nature.

The adults are unable to understand what has happened, and when, that night, they see Eustace running around the terrace of the inn where they are all staying, "saluting, praising, and blessing the great forces and manifestations of Nature" (p. 28), they trap him and put him into the prison of his room. And there, says the Italian servingboy, Gennaro, he will die. Gennaro is the only one who realizes what has happened to Eustace. "Ho capito," he says to him when the picnickers return to the inn, and he announces later that he is alive "because I had neither parents nor relatives nor friends, so that, when

the first night came, I could run through the woods, and climb
the rocks, and plung into the water, until I had accomplished
my desire!" (p. 36). The desire, that is, to be one with the
secret, swarming, vital nature Eustace describes, to pass through
and beyond the obstacles society erects to keep itself safe from
the knowledge of Pan, the frightening awareness of what it is
like to be young. The oppositions of the novels between the
room and the view, between England and Italy, between the
spectator and the participant are here concentrated, even more
explicitly than in "The Celestial Omnibus," into the conflict
of youth and age.

For that reason, Gennaro is the most interesting character
in the story. There is no place for him in either of the opposed
camps. Already past the magic age, but not completely past,
already a part of the adult world, but not completely a part,
he is uncomfortably situated with a foot in each. Gennaro is
the only one who can communicate with both Eustace and the
adults, and he falls victim to his double vision. Both Judas and
Jesus, he first betrays Eustace to captivity and then, with a
second and better thought, saves him, dying, as Rickie does for
Stephen in *The Longest Journey*, so Eustace may live. Eustace
is last seen fleeing into the trees—"looking like a great white
moth" (p. 38)—from the artificiality, the hypocrisy, and the
coerciveness of society. But his triumph, which is otherwise so
reminiscent of the boy's or Evelyn's, is in large part muted by
Gennaro's less fantastic escape into death and away from the
inevitable tragedy of growing old. The superiority of "The Story
of a Panic" to most of the other tales in the volume derives
precisely from Forster's ambiguous attitude toward the ideal he
presents: available to all (Pan), it can be grasped only by a few
and by those few, it would seem, only for a while. The last
sounds of the story are "the shouts and the laughter of the escaping boy" (p. 38), but Gennaro's body remains, and with it
an undertone of dissatisfaction and even of disbelief in Eustace's
easy evasion of the claims of this world.

It is Gennaro's unhappy fate to see his "vision" fade, as
Wordsworth put it, "into the light of common day." "The Road
from Colonus" picks up this theme and develops it at length
in the story of Mr. Lucas, the oldest and most world-weary of

Forster's heroes. Mr. Lucas comes to Greece to fulfill the dream
of a lifetime, only to find that everything he sees is banal and
dull. He is, he admits to himself, a man who is growing old,
"and it made no difference whether that man looked at the
Thames or the Eurotas" (p. 127). The subtlety of the story
lies in the fact that here, for the first time, prison is an image
not simply of society's disapproval but also of a subjective,
psychological state. Mr. Lucas is the prisoner of age: "His
phrases and gestures had become stiff and set. . . . There was
nothing and no one to blame: he was simply growing old"
(p. 127).

Mr. Lucas does, however, recognize his state; he knows
that he is discontented, and, as he says to himself, "I do mind
being old, and I will pretend no longer" (p. 128), he has an experience that releases him from the confinements of age and
sets his struggling spirit free. In a tree whose hollowness en-
closes a religious shrine and a symbolically redemptive stream,
he comes to the end of what Lionel Trilling has called "the
romantic quest," the perception of "coherence in nature's apparently 'accidental pattern.' " [3] More than that, in Mr. Lucas'
revelation Forster comes closer than he usually does to defining
being as the denial or loss of the self. Standing on a rock within
the tree, above the hidden source of the stream, he has "the
strange feeling of one who is moving, yet at peace—the feeling
of the swimmer, who, after long struggling with chopping seas,
finds that after all the tide will sweep him to his goal." He is
"conscious only of the stream below his feet, and that all things
were a stream in which he was moving" (p. 130). Mr. Lucas'
experience is essentially mystical, and in his timeless apprehension of the unity of all things, in his selfless indentification with
the great stream on which all things flow, he dies to the ordinary
world and in losing his life, finds it.

Even before he stepped into the tree, Mr. Lucas had wished
for independence from the other members of his party. Now
his desire is consummated. But unlike Harold or Evelyn or the
boy, he is at the same time still a part of ordinary life, and unlike the curate, who undergoes an expansion rather than a

3 Trilling, E. M. Forster (Norfolk, Conn.: New Directions, 1943),
p. 40.

contraction of personality in the ordinary sense, he is puzzled how to bring the ideal into fruitful contact with the real. His lot, as we have seen, is most like Gennaro's, but Forster in this case refuses to provide the easy answer of death. The situation that results is the most tragic, or at least the most pathetic, in *The Celestial Omnibus*. The others catch up with him, and he finds not only that their enthusiasm is insincere, but even that he himself is unable to express what he feels. The phrases and gestures remain stiff and conventional, and he realizes he may lose all he has gained: "He no longer trusted himself to journey through the world, for old thoughts, old wearinesses might be waiting to rejoin him as soon as he left the shade of the planes" (p. 132).

And so he proposes that they spend the night there, for "one such night would place him beyond relapse, and confirm him for ever in the kingdom he had regained" (p. 132). It soon becomes clear, however, that the others, despite their effusions over Colonus, intend to go on. The outcome of the battle of wills that ensues is inevitable; Mr. Lucas is adamant, but society is strong, and when his daughter fails to move him with her arguments, she has him moved bodily onto his mule. Once again Mr. Lucas is a prisoner, and the whole party departs, on its way back to England. When last seen, Mr. Lucas is back in his home, a querulous and petty old man complaining, in unconscious parody of his experience at Colonus, about "the water gurgling in the pipe above my head." "There's nothing I dislike more than running water" (p. 140), he announces, and the horror of his transformation reaches its climax. Nothing touches him now, except his own comforts, and he is unmoved even by his daughter's discovery that on the night he had wished to pass at Colonus, a large tree blew down, ruining everything around it, killing several people, even causing the stream to change its course. When Ethel comments unctuously on the tragedy: "Such a marvellous deliverance does make one believe in Providence" (p. 143), the irony of the story is complete. For Mr. Lucas, it is implied, had better have died himself, since now he is worse than dead: body without spirit, life without meaning. He has descended into the trivial abyss he so much feared from the peak of his momentary vision. The reader has

been invited throughout the tale to draw an ironic comparison
between Mr. Lucas and his daughter and their heroic prototypes,
Oedipus and Antigone, and now, as "The Road from Colonus"
ends, he is painfully reminded of Oedipus' death:

> For he was taken without lamentation,
> Illness or suffering; indeed his end
> Was wonderful if mortal's ever was.[4]

Mr. Lucas' fate substitutes for Gennaro's death a state of
death-in-life and so forces the conclusion that most of the other
stories shirk: that in the actual confrontation of the ideal with
the real, the ideal has little chance of success. It is the fault of
those other tales that they simulate a victory which is no victory
at all, that they evade the problem that has been posed and so
sacrifice artistic integrity to wishful thinking. The forces are
massed, but the battle is never joined; fantasy simply runs off
the field, announcing, with more enthusiasm than reason, that
it has won the day. "The Road from Colonus" deserves its key
position as the last story in the volume, and not only because
it accepts its own implications but also because, for the first
time, one is convinced that the ideal is the real. One believes
in Harold's Greece only if one is willing to accept anything
classical as necessarily good; Other Kingdom is credible to the
degree that mythology evokes the expected response in the
reader. But it is possible to believe in Mr. Lucas' vision because
one believes in him.

Mr. Lucas, then, stands out in these stories as a "round"
character, but how significant is his fate? How significant can it
be when he manages so much more easily to evade the prison
of his own old age than the confining grip of his daughter. The
stories raise, in other words, questions not only of artistic integrity, but of artistic value as well. When Dickens speaks, in
Little Dorrit, of "the prison of this lower world," he is after
something much more significant than the Circumlocution Of-
fice, with its vast jungle of red tape; he is concerned with what
it is like to be human in this world at any time. This is not to

---

4 The quotation is from Robert Fitzgerald's translation of Oedipus
at Colonus in The Complete Greek Tragedies, II (Chicago: University of
Chicago Press, 1959), p. 150.

say that Forster's problems and concerns (the letter versus the spirit, say) are unimportant ones, but that, in *The Celestial Omnibus*, he picks them up by their smallest ends. Therefore his early stories have an unmistakable period flavor that Dickens' novel, for all its saturation in the Victorian age, does not. The evils of "The Story of a Panic" and "The Other Side of the Hedge" are local and, in the long run, temporary. It is the surface of society, not the human depth, that Forster reaches in his first collection, and in the stories, as in the novels, it is only when he allows himself to peer into the abyss that his fiction passes from its Edwardian dichotomies to the richer dialectic of the modern world.

The Eternal Moment is a much more uneven collection than its predecessor, containing as it does Forster's best as well as his least successful story. It is also, in mood and theme, a less homogeneous collection and therefore more difficult to make generalizations about. It has already been suggested that the stories are, on the whole, gloomier and more melancholy than those in *The Celestial Omnibus*; there are even moments in the later volume when Forster's tone comes close, in its bitterness, to cynicism and despair. The prison becomes a more frightening and a more all-encompassing image as its power is seen to derive less from the impositions of society on the imaginative and nonconforming individual than from some inherent flaw in the nature of humanity or of life itself. Equally, the solutions that the stories offer change with the problems they raise. The viability of an "other kingdom," at least in the form in which it is presented in *The Celestial Omnibus*, is increasingly, though not always intentionally, called into doubt. There are still two worlds in most of these tales, but they are sometimes different in content from what they were earlier, and in any case the lines between them are less sharply drawn. The possibility of moments of vision and insight into a better way of life remain, but retreat into a hypostatic world of values is now the exception rather than the rule. In other words there is, in these later tales, a partial but significant movement away from conventional mythology and Hellenism, from the facile primitivism of the earlier book. Answers, where they are given, are more tentative;

hope, where there is any, is more equivocal; truth, though it saves, is less comforting, and may even destroy.

None of the stories in *The Eternal Moment* conforms exactly to this pattern, but "The Point of It" comes close to expressing the central spirit of the collection. Like *The Longest Journey* and unlike most of the tales, it has both a protagonist and a hero, who between them illustrate the theme of Wordsworth's "Intimations of Immortality" ode: "Shades of the prison-house begin to close/Upon the growing Boy." Michael, whose life is treated at length in the story, represents the passing of "the visionary gleam," while Harold, who appears infrequently, is meant to suggest the "perpetual benediction" that "the thought of our past years . . . doth breed." Forster's reworking of the ode is naturally different in many respects from the poem itself: the atmosphere of the story is more acrid, its tone, sentimental and ironic by turns, less assured. One feels that, as in *The Longest Journey*, Forster is struggling with a personal problem and that in his two leading characters he has embodied, on the one hand, his sense of dissatisfaction with himself and, on the other, his idealized projection of what he would have liked to be. The results are the same in the story as in the novel, and they help to explain why Forster does better at reproducing Wordsworth's sense of loss than his consolations. Harold, who bears a strong resemblance to Stephan Wonham, shares, as we shall see, his inadequacies as a symbol of the ideal. It is Michael who, suggesting like Rickie a self-portrait, gains our interest and our credence.

Forster summarizes Michael's career with great subtlety. At the start, we are made to like and admire the young man, and rightly so: "He cared for the universe, for the tiny tangle in it that we call civilization, for his fellow-men who had made the tangle and who transcended it" (p. 203). His impulses are good, he is filled with concern for humanity, and, under the guidance of his future wife, who, as Michael himself recognizes, balances his belief in love with a belief in truth, he enters on his career of doing good for humanity. Soon, however, Forster begins to undercut his protagonist, to destroy his praises with a suggestion of irony: his work with the British Museum (his noble aspirations have been channeled into the Home Civil

Service) is "rather notable" (p. 204); his marriage is "sufficiently happy" (p. 205); and as for his temper, "he grew sweeter every day" (p. 205). It becomes increasingly clear that Michael's tolerance and sympathy are in reality faults rather than virtues and that his success is a direct outcome of his mediocrity. As he grows older, Michael, or Sir Michael, as he is now, becomes more benign, more conciliatory, and even more religious. "This life," he thinks, "is a preparation for the next. . . . Experience is the great teacher; blessed are the experienced, for they need not further modify their ideals" (p. 210).

Michael is right; his life is a preparation for the next, but his reward is very different from what he expects. He wakes, after his death, to find himself in hell, a vast, sandy plain suggesting "the universe as old age" (p. 214). It is in Forster's description of the afterlife that the full horror of his story becomes apparent, for, as Michael learns, "the fault was his, but the fate humanity's." "The Point of It," then, is less an indictment of one man's life than a bitter account of what happens to all men. There are two hells, one for the soft and one for the hard, since "the years are bound either to liquefy a man or to stiffen him, and . . . Love and Truth, who seem to contend for our souls like angels, hold each the seeds of our decay" (p. 218). In "Albergo Empedocle," Harold might have been saved by truth and love, but in the universe of this later story they are helpless against humanity's inevitable decay. Michael's wife lies in the hell of the hard, and with her "the reformers and ascetics and all sword-like souls"; in the hell of the soft, there are not only "the sentimentalists, the conciliators, the peacemakers," but also "the humanists, and all who have trusted the warmer vision" (p. 218).

With the inclusion of the humanists, one begins to feel how comprehensive Forster's vision of man's fate is in this story. Humanism, after all, is the creed of his most sympathetic heroes and heroines, and, as so many of his essays attest ("What I Believe" is a notable example), it was and has continued to be his own. But in the oppressive atmosphere of "The Point of It" no one escapes the hell of experience, no one, at any rate, who is subject to the inexorable passage of time. Only one character is not, and that is the hero, Harold, who appears, first as boy and then as boy-angel, at the beginning and end of the tale. The center of the story, in fact, lies at its extreme edges, for, although Michael holds the stage longer, he is, in terms of the ideal, merely a foil to Harold. As the story opens, both boys are down at the sea, where Harold is supposed to be recuperating and Michael (now Micky) looking after him. Harold's great moment comes while he is rowing and when Michael, forgetting his solicitousness in a rush of high spirits, urges his friend to "bust" himself. "He was," Forster comments, "approaching the mystic state that is the athlete's true though unacknowledged goal: he was beginning to be" (p. 200). And his being is consummated directly, as his heart fails and he dies with one hand "plunged deep into the sea" (p. 202). The symbolism is clear: Harold, passing through the redemptive waters, joins Evelyn, Eustace, and the others in Other Kingdom, which finally receives its proper name—the kingdom of death. He escapes, not like the others from the burdensome weight of society, but from the suffocating requirements of life itself.

Michael's tragedy is not, as Mr. Lucas' is, the choice of the wrong path but of any path at all. When he compares himself with his dead friend to his own advantage, he is, despite Harold's energy, youth, and determination, justified; he is a better, a finer, a more intelligent person. But he lives, and there, in all its harrowing simplicity, lies his tragedy. His decline has already been traced. Even at the time, he does not quite understand the point of Harold's action, and as the years pass, the memory of his friend passes with them. In hell he is reminded once again, when he hears the voice of some heavenly spirit of being: " 'I was before choice,' came the song. 'I was before hardness and softness were divided. I was in the days when truth was love. And I am' " (p. 221). As Michael listens to the spirit's Wordsworthian enticements, he remembers, or at least desires to remember, his youth, and he dies a second death, after which he finds himself once more being rowed, this time by an Angelic Harold over the infernal stream. He hears "a voice say, 'The point of it . . .' and a weight fell off his body and he crossed mid-stream" (p. 224). He is back in a landscape that recalls exactly the scene of the opening pages, and he is saved.

But what does it mean to say that Michael is saved? It

may be naïve to point out that Michael is already dead and that in a story where heaven and hell are simply metaphors and not theological entities, such salvation is only a bitter irony, but it is true nonetheless. Or does the story mean, more simply, to express an ideal that ought to be realized in this life, an ideal that asks man to retain into adulthood the spirit of youth? In other words, is Michael's encounter with Harold analogous to the curate's with the faun or Eustace's with Pan? This seems more likely: the curious reproduction at the end of the story of its first scene suggests that Michael might have been saved as a youth if he had at that time seen the point of it. But then it must be said that Forster is too successful in showing the inevitable decay involved in the process of aging. The brilliance of the story lies in Forster's ability to make Michael a symbol of all men, its failure, in his inability to make Harold a believable symbol of any kind. The failure is particularly significant. The primitivist heroes of *The Eternal Moment* are sketchier than their counterparts in the earlier volume. Without the abundant woods and trees and streams of *The Celestial Omnibus*, there is no place for them. As one moves from the first to the second collection, the *genius loci*, the sense of place, gives way to the sense of time, and the eternal heavens and kingdoms, the refuges of Evelyn and the others, cease to represent the ideal. It is not in space but in time that hope is made credible in *The Eternal Moment*, and then, as in the last two novels, it is in an ambiguous future of expectation and desire, sufficiently vague to be believed in, too distant to be denied.

Several years ago Forster published an essay in which he wrote: "Growing old is an emotion which comes over us at almost any age. I had it myself between the ages of twenty-five and thirty, and still possess a diary recording my despair." [5] "The Point of It" would seem to be another expression of that despair, but its interest is not simply biographical. In its concern with time and age, in its redefinition of life itself as a prison, it is symptomatic of the collection as a whole. Two of the other stories in particular develop the latter theme. Both are less complex than "The Point of It" and can be dealt with

5 "De Senectute," *The London Magazine*, IV (November, 1957), 15–16.

quickly. "The Machine Stops" is an overly long and overly explicit meditation (to use the narrator's word) on the society of the future, the "scientific" world toward which the road on the wrong side of the hedge was tending. Man, served by a myriad of switches and buttons that cater to his every wish and make movement virtually unnecessary, now lives in a vast confining network of underground rooms. From one isolated cell to another communication is carried on through the elaborate apparatus of the machine, which "did not transmit *nuances* of expression. It only gave a general idea of people—an idea that was good enough for all practical purposes" (p. 148).

The machine is Forster's "brave new world," his story, as he has said, "a counterblast to one of the heavens of H. G. Wells" (pp. vii–viii). The civilization Forster describes is one in which man's servant has become his master, his jailer, in which means have so seriously been mistaken for ends that ultimately the machine is accepted as an object of religious veneration. Against this idolatry, this uniformity and second-handedness, Forster sets his misfit hero, Kuno, who expounds repeatedly and at length the story's message: "Man is the measure" (p. 167). It is Kuno who, alone among his atrophied and barely human fellows, values the body, he who discovers that a bare handful of men and women still live above the ground, he who predicts, as the machine collapses, the rebirth of a new and humanistic civilization from this remnant.

Forster has said that "The Machine Stops" stands "quite apart from all [his] other work." [6] and in some ways it does: for the first time the "real" world of humanity represents the ideal, while the foreground of the story is given over to an uncharacteristically Kafkaesque distortion of the ordinary into the fantastic. The metaphorical transmutation of a rigid and sterile society into a machine is suggestive; unfortunately, Forster does not go far enough; the tale remains too schematic, too fanciful (rather than fantastic), too didactic. As Forster's allegorical tract for his times, the story suffers by comparison with the multitude of other inverted utopias this century has produced. In other respects, "The Machine Stops" strongly resembles the

6 In a letter to this writer, dated June 24, 1958.

rest of the tales; its theme, its values, and its dominant image are characteristic. "Isolation," Forster has recently written, "means death. And isolation sometimes masks itself behind bustle or worldly success or what passes for civilization." [7] "The Machine Stops" is Forster's comment on the human failure to communicate and his plea for a change of heart, but the unconvincing conversion of Kuno's mother before her death and Kuno's own wistful belief in "tomorrow—" (p. 197) belie the hope that is meant to be suggested at the last.

Though its image of society as a prison is gloomier, more elaborate, and more inclusive than any in *The Celestial Omnibus*, "The Machine Stops" shares to a degree with the stories in that volume a feeling that man's condition is not inevitable. It is possible, in other words, to imagine a change in the social context that would allow Kuno or others like him to realize their ideals. In "Mr. Andrews," a far shorter but more suggestive tale, which also deals with the themes of isolation and communication, the stress is once again, as in "The Point of It," on the imperfections in the very nature of things. In addition, "Mr. Andrews" resembles "The Machine Stops" in being (in part) an allegory. As such, the story constitutes a satire on anthropomorphism. The hero of the tale arrives in heaven to find a whole series of gods who are the merest reflections of the imaginings of men on earth. As the hopes and wishes and beliefs of men change, so change the gods. And if there is a lesson implicit in the satire, it is probably, as in "The Machine Stops," that man is the measure, that in the train of the gods follow disappointment and frustration.

But there is more to the story than this. To a large degree it anticipates, without fully recognizing the implications of, the dilemma posed by *A Passage to India*: the necessity for discovering an order neither so rigid as to erect artificial barriers between men nor so all-embracing as to be only another name for chaos. In the sandwichlike structure of the tale, the middle section is devoted to the problem of exclusion. Mr. Andrews' heaven proves to be a parody of human society, with its sects and coteries and cliques, and there he learns the folly of desiring to

7 "Introduction" to Donald Windham's *The Warm Country* (New York: Charles Scribner's Sons, n.d.), p. 9.

reproduce his "glorious individual life on earth" in "an individual life to come" (p. 225). Individuality, he finds, is a curse, and his loneliness weighs on him all the more heavily for his remembrance of his meeting with the Turk outside the gates of heaven, when each prayed the other might enter. The separateness of heaven is set against the moment of contact brought about by the selflessness of the two men, but even this, it would seem, is not enough to overcome the obstacles which divide men from one another. The curiously impersonal personal relationship between Mr. Andrews and the Turk is not repeated, but it provides the first step toward the total abnegation of identity: as the two disappointed men leave heaven, selflessness gives way to a literal loss of self, and Mr. Andrews and his friend become one with the world soul.

In a sense, the two men undergo a second death, but it would be misleading to compare the incident too closely with the analogous one in "The Point of It." While Michael's movement is retrograde, magically re-entering, as he does, a state he has, or seems to have, definitively left behind, theirs is the logical completion of a progression away from confinement and constriction; fulfillment lies in complete identification with the "allness" of the world soul. No symbol in the earlier stories is so radical in its implications as this one. Neither Michael's nor Mr. Lucas' apprehension and experience of being excludes our awareness that it is they who are having the experience. Some remnant of personality remains. Not so in this story, for at the end there *is* no Mr. Andrews, no Turk, only a vast, mystical sausage grinder with a taste for humanity. It is not a thought one would expect Forster to find particularly comforting: however capacious, there is no room in the world soul for humanism. And indeed, the last lines attempt, factitiously and unconvincingly, to introduce a note of consolation by suggesting that the two men not only pass into the world soul but also make it better. But this last-minute attempt to personalize the great void fails to disguise the fact that being in "Mr. Andrews" is no longer a state whose virtues are translatable back into the unregenerate world, as it is by implication in the earlier tales, but a negation of everything, good equally with bad, in that world. The moment of contact between the two men, which is the high point of the story, is submerged along with the pettiness of heaven, and one has to push only a little further to see in total inclusion a symbol of the abyss of indistinction over which all man's structures rest so uneasily. This, as has been indicated, Forster does in his last novel, where the opposite extremes of order become the Scylla and Charybdis between which man has to steer his difficult course.

The aftermath of Mr. Andrews' meeting with his friend makes particularly, if unintentionally, ironic the title of the collection as a whole: *The Eternal Moment*. Forster's conception of time is expressed most succinctly in *Aspects of the Novel*, where he writes: "Daily life, whatever it may be really, is practically composed of two lives—the life in time and the life by values—and our conduct reveals a double allegiance" (p. 30). In "The Point of It," Michael's memory of Harold's death and his understanding of its significance are swamped by the life in time; in "Mr. Andrews," the life by values can only resist its encroachments by ceasing to exist altogether. In both, the "great moments," which heretofore have brought illumination or salvation to Forster's heroes, are instead the beginning points of a pathetic decline. It is true that, even in the early works, the concentration on discrete moments implies an awareness that on all sides of them stretches the life in time, dull and prosaic, never completely to be forgotten. But in the later fiction, where the moments themselves become more tenuous, this awareness grows, and the stories in *The Eternal Moment*, however else they differ from one another, are agreed on the difficulty of maintaining an allegiance to the life by values while continuing to exist in the monotonous and uninspired life of everyday.

This is true even of "Co-ordination," the gayest and least typical of these stories. At first sight the tale appears to be much closer in spirit to the earlier collection, particularly to "The Celestial Omnibus," with which it shares both heavenly background and theme. In the basic contrast between the mechanically coordinated school system, which produces discord in music and between people, and the coordination "through the central sources of Melody and Victory" (p. 244), which is achieved when the characters penetrate beneath the artificial form and surface of school life, one finds again Dante's opposition of the letter and the spirit. As in "Albergo Empedocle," there is a moment of truth for both Miss Haddon and the principal of the school, and as in "The Story of a Panic" or "The Curate's Friend," the moment springs from a redemptive contact with nature. Both women, as they raise the seashell to their ears, reach, in their different ways, "the central sources." The sea that Miss Haddon hears whispering, chattering, echoing, and singing for joy and the forest through which the principal imagines herself to be riding with her friends suggest the possibility of communication, and that possibility is realized the next day when the two women kiss. Moreover, the happy aftereffects of their experience are even more fully and more successfully articulated than in many of the earlier tales. The picnic at which the schoolgirls play totally disorganized games, like the cavalry band which earlier sends them "off their heads with joy" (p. 237), is not only the comically human equivalent of the victory (or in the other case, of the melody) which is decreed in heaven, but also Forster's joyous symbol of "the mess that comes of life" (WAFTT, p. 142).

Despite all of these resemblances, however, "Co-ordination" appropriately takes its place among the later tales. Miss Haddon, sad, spinsterish, and ineffectual, is older and wearier than any of the protagonists of The Celestial Omnibus except Mr. Lucas, and though like him she is aware of how false her life has become, she lacks the vigor of his determination "to die fighting" (p. 128). Time and age weigh even more heavily on her than on him, and when her moment comes it is, significantly, at second hand. Her vision is not directly of the coherence of all things around her but (through the medium of the shell) of the sea that is associated with her sailor-father and her own childhood. It is retrospective and wistful, and though Forster intimates that her experience will remain with her forever, he can think of no better way of symbolizing her new life than by sending her off to a melancholy isolation by the sea, away from the school, away from the enthusiastic girls, and away from her brief communication with the principal. There seems to be, after all, little to choose between the long waste of Miss Haddon's past and the doubtful happiness of her future.

One is tempted, as so often before, to look beyond the confines of the tale, not because problems have been left unresolved but because Forster creates the false impression that everything has been tidied up. "Co-ordination" comes close to convincing us: written, like *A Room with a View*, with verve and gusto, it almost triumphs, as that novel does, through sheer high spirits. Not quite, however: Raphael has the last word, but Mephistopheles may after all be right in supposing that he has witnessed the complete breakdown of order. The most troublesome question that Forster raises in his story is one of means and ends, and it is the one whose implications he dodges most completely. "How does one most effectively reach the spirit which inspired Beethoven's 'Eroica'?" the story asks, and it answers: "not by 'thumping' at the piano but by listening to a cavalry band." The answer is based upon the same sentimental and uncritical assumption that mars so much of Forster's earlier work, namely, that the simple destruction of factitious order is enough to bring about true order and understanding. But is it? When Beethoven asks his clerk whether the girls perform with insight, the answer is, or obviously should be, no; the regimental music and the picnic are in the nature of a saturnalia, a relief from Miss Haddon's weary teaching. But what, one asks, will happen the next day, when the girls, willy-nilly, return to their thumping? Will they then play with insight? It seems unlikely. In other words, the treats provided by Beethoven and Napoleon are only half the answer: the exuberant destruction of the sham and the fake; conceived as ends in themselves, as in effect they are, the picnic and the band become symbols of a disorder fully as sterile as the principal's coordinative system. The necessary distinction between the order that kills and the order that, by providing the legitimate and requisite form for insight, saves, is not made.

Forster comments in *Aspects of the Novel* that "Dickens causes his characters to vibrate a little, so that they borrow his life and appear to lead one of their own. It is a conjuring trick" (p. 69). The statement has doubtful validity when applied to Dickens, but it is a good description of what Forster is doing in "Co-ordination." The characters laugh and run and talk, but all the while they are being pulled about and manipulated to prove a point. The result is that the story's structure is as imperfect as its assumptions are faulty; it suffers, in fact, from too much coordination. One must, of course, accept the fact that the various events of the story follow on Beethoven's and Napoleon's decrees, but while the band and the shell are plausible translations of melody into human terms and the picnic, of victory, the legacy that Miss Haddon so conveniently receives is too patently a *deus ex machina* even for a story full of heavenly interventions. Moreover, it is Forster who unceremoniously disposes of all the human characters after the outing, transferring the final scene to heaven, where, *sub specie aeternitatis* presumably, the earthly happenings are explained.

But it is here that the element of contrivance in the story is most apparent. Raphael is Forster's spokesman, Mephistopheles his strawman in this pasteboard heaven, but Mephistopheles has a better case than the angel allows, better than he himself realizes, for the reader at least remains doubtful about the exact meaning of "the central sources" and even more doubtful about what effect their experiences have had on Miss Haddon and the girls. It is perhaps the prerogative of angels alone to be more lyrical than logical, for though Forster's legerdemain is skillful, it is not skillful enough to keep the reader from a backward glance to Ellen and Mildred thumping for a new mistress and to Miss Haddon, still old and still alone. One would like to have heard Mephistopheles on the subject!

The creaking celestial machinery of "Co-ordination" has no place in the very different story, "The Eternal Moment," where the heroine, Miss Raby, is forced to work out her substantial problems in exclusively human terms. There are no heavenly agents here to bring the great moment about, no miraculous shells or bequests to provide an easy transition from the life in time to the life by values, no fantastic other kingdoms to provide a permanent refuge from the inadequacies of personal relations or from the encroachments of old age. The two worlds of the other stories appear now not as discrete and polar entities but as different, though coexistent, levels of the mind. Consequently, Miss Raby is more fully realized than any of her fellow protagonists, while the narrator, for once, is less concerned with pointing facile morals than with probing psychological and moral complexities.

Miss Raby can best be imagined as Caroline Abbott twenty years later. The central incident of her life—Feo's proposal on the mountainside—suggests Caroline's encounters with Gino: both women fall in love, both avoid physical consummation of their love, both have instead an experience of the values the two men represent, and both are better as a result of their transitory contacts. But Miss Raby is unaware of what has happened to her. Never acknowledged, her love works subconsiously as the directing force of her life, making possible her career as a novelist and stimulating her need to break down barriers, to connect and join the classes, and especially to give herself away. In a sense, Miss Raby is constantly trying to relive her great moment, indirectly attempting to realize what was left unconsummated. As a result, her life, though on the whole successful, has an element of frustration in it, and it is this frustration that eventually brings her back to Vorta.

The opening lines of Dante's *Inferno*, which Forster has Gino quote in *Where Angels Fear to Tread*, are an exact description of her situation: Miss Raby is lost in a dark wood of confusion and irresolution. Middle-aged, faced with the prospect of becoming old, the balance of her life is upset. Everything about her, in fact, suggests a precarious midpoint between irreconcilable extremes; the strength of the eternal moment is no longer sufficient to keep the underground stream flowing, not at least while it remains buried. Despite the ideas, values, and attitudes that she expresses and that make her so sympathetic, there is something cold and aggressive in her actual relations with people, something shrill and abstract in her desire to be egalitarian, a touch of Miss Lavish in her romantic idealization of self-exposure. At this critical moment in her life she finds in Vorta, with its mixture of Teuton and Latin, with its contrast between an aggressively modern civilization and the vestiges of a more primitive and virile community, a symbolic reflection of her ambivalence.

Her initial reluctance to return to the town, her fear that she will find it changed, and her disproportionate guilt for what she feels she has done to Vorta by popularizing it in her first novel are all responses to more basic anxieties: in fact, she is reluctant to encounter her present self, fearful of discovering her past, guilty for having used Feo simply as an instrument of her own growth. Her movement through the village—from the new hotel to the old inn and finally to Feo himself—must be read as a compulsive journey back in time, to the conscious recognition of her love and to the awareness "that the incident upon the mountain had been one of the great moments of her life—perhaps the greatest, certainly the most enduring" (p. 300). Miss Raby's pathetic and ludicrous effort to get possession of one of Feo's children and her attempt to find out whether he did love her twenty years before are the direct outcome of this awareness and of her simultaneous understanding that she no longer loves him: frightened by what she has learned, she tries one last time to make contact on the human level. But, as she hears that the campanile, the one beautiful thing that has come of her worldly success, is sinking, she finds that her gesture is futile, that there is no connecting with the world of action and change.

It is at this point that the central critical questions of the story seem to emerge: is Miss Raby a failure?—and does her life illustrate, as one critic has put it in speaking of "the moral power exerted by the 'symbolic moment' . . . the disastrous effects which follow its denial"? [8] The fact is that the story itself refuses to answer these questions unambiguously. Less concerned with passing judgment than with exploring the complicated relation between life and art, "The Eternal Moment" is Forster's closest approach to a Joycean portrait of the artists, a description of how and why the artist is different from his fellow men. Consequently, there is no discontinuity in Miss Raby's personality before and after her revelation. Her greatest discovery is neither of her love nor of its end, but of a justification for the life she has led: she knows now not only that she did not seize her moment but, more important, that, given what she was and is, she could not have seized it. "She saw that she had lived worthily," the narrator comments. "She was conscious

8 Frederick P. W. McDowell, "Forster's 'Natural Supernaturalism': The Tales," *Modern Fiction Studies*, VII (Autumn, 1961), 274.

of a triumph over experience and earthly facts, a triumph magnificent, cold, hardly human, whose existence no one but herself would ever surmise" (p. 307).

A similar passage at the end of *Where Angels Fear to Tread* suggests that Philip Herriton has fallen short of the ideal of involvement, but the effect is different here: there is no doubt that Miss Raby shares with Philip, Rickie, and others the aesthetic view of life; her triumph is cold, almost inhuman, but the characteristic irony or disapproval are muted. Indeed, Colonel Leyland's betrayal of Miss Raby at the end serves not only to make her victory still lonelier but also to confirm our sympathies for her and for the life she has led. The point is that the story does not stress the usual Forsterian opposition of the spectator and the participant. The focus here is on Miss Raby as a woman who values what she cannot herself do or be and who is, perhaps *faute de mieux*, an artist.

The temptation to read the story as Forster's explanation and partial justification of his own life and, as a consequence, of his artistic vocation is strong. Certainly there are striking resemblances between Miss Raby and her creator, and it cannot be fortuitous that the title of her novel is not only the title of Forster's story but also of the volume in which it appears. Forster himself was just beginning his career as an artist and had then entered upon the five-year period during which he felt himself to be growing old. "The Eternal Moment," like the later fiction, is full of the awareness of change, flux, and transcience. Vorta, Feo, the campanile are all works of time, and all prove less permanent than the values that have informed Miss Raby's writing and that have given even to her life something of the stability of a work of art. As Miss Raby looks down "on the perishing and perishable beauty of the valley" that seems to her now "to be infinitely distant" (p. 307), she accepts her life without guilt and the coming of old age without regret. She understands now that in having lived the eternal moment, even without full awareness, she has, as woman and artist, found, if not the ideal or even the best, then at least a worthy and workable answer to the disorder of daily life.

It is also a more honest answer than the one that is given in "Co-ordination." Perhaps inevitably, given Forster's premises, that is, his sense of life as a difficult and generally disappointing affair, the best of his tales are those which, to some degree at least, end unhappily. Miss Raby leaving the room unnoticed while her companions stay behind to keep up appearances is a more adequate symbol than Miss Haddon inviting her former pupils to visit her at the shore. "The Eternal Moment" is a story of compromise and acceptance, and it acknowledges, even while claiming a victory for Miss Raby, that she has lost something too. The world itself is unchanged and Miss Raby, however distantly, remains part of it; or rather, she is in it but not of it, as solitary and lonely, one feels, as she is triumphant. Unlike the early stories, "The Eternal Moment" accepts this ambiguous situation, and that may be the reason why, despite its date, Forster chose to include it in his second collection, where, even among these later efforts, it stands unrivaled for its honesty and maturity—except by "The Story of the Siren," the latest and most satisfactory of Forster's tales.

This story, though it is a fantasy, has none of the inadequacies of Forster's other work in the genre. The Siren of the title has more in common with modern philosophy than with classical mythology, and as symbol she is more at home in the world of Sartre than in Wordsworth's. The sea in which she makes her home is a far stranger place than the gentle streams and estuaries of the earlier stories. The "always changing" (p. 249) waters of "The Story of the Siren" provide no easy passage to primitivist values; rather, they are the frightening reality that, in its indifference to man and his works, surrounds him and threatens his very existence. When Giuseppe, the protagonist of the tale, dives into them, he becomes "like a piece of the sea" (p. 252), but his experience of "being" is very different from Harold's or Mr. Lucas': there is no angelic bliss for him, no revelation of coherence and beauty. In seeing the Siren, Giuseppe has a vision of what today would be called man's existential predicament—existence in a world without intrinsic value, without meaning, without necessary form, a world in which everything passes, changes, and dies. Plunging into the waters, Giuseppe discovers the truth that underlies man's attempts to order his universe, and, as events prove, it is a truth man does not willingly admit.

It is no accident that the chief villains of the piece are priests, since it is they, Forster implies, who do most to impose on the world of contingency and mortality a factitious structure, they who "have blessed the air, so [the Siren] cannot breathe it, and blessed the rocks, so that she cannot sit on them" (p. 249). Religion is man's breakwater against the flood of his fear, and behind it he builds his imaginary castle that is in fact his prison. No image of constraint in the earlier stories—not the prison of society in "The Machine Stops," not the prison of age in "The Point of It," not the prison of selfhood in "Mr. Andrews"—is more inclusive than the "silence and loneliness" (p. 258) of which Giuseppe's brother speaks. Nowhere in the stories is communication more minimal, nowhere is there less joy, nowhere are people so cruel and so frightened, for there is no escape from the Siren, and in banishing her to the sea, man simply lets in by the back door the dread and anxiety he is at such pains to conceal from himself. Only by facing his condition, the story suggests, can man save and liberate himself from the senselessness of his existence.

"Death destroys a man: the idea of Death saves him," one of the characters in *Howards End* thinks, and it is essentially this belief that underlies "The Story of the Siren." The Siren, in other words, is not herself death, as Professor Trilling has said,[9] for then her appearance above the water, which is predicted in the course of the story, would mean the end of the world or salvation only in superhuman terms. She is, rather, the truth that may set man free in this life, and Forster, as usual, is more hopeful than assured about its realization. Giuseppe's great moment is a grim one: the truth is too new and too large for him; he is overburdened by what he has learned and unable to take the next step, which is Forster's desideratum. Even his marriage to a woman who has also seen the Siren is not enough to change him. "They loved each other," his brother says, "but love is not happiness. We can all get love. Love is nothing" (p. 253). Love is nothing because truth is greater, and truth must be for all men. Without it communication is at best makeshift. Giuseppe is cut off from his fellow men

9 Trilling, *E. M. Forster*, p. 43.

because of their willful blindness, and without their help he is unable to emerge from the abyss.

Hope, such as it is, lies, characteristically, in the future, with his child. Characteristically again, though paradoxically, the boy is presented in religious terms: the son of Joseph and Mary (Giuseppe and Maria), he is Forster's humanistic savior, "who will fetch up the Siren from the sea, and destroy silence, and save the world!" (p. 258). The whole of the tale works up to and then away from the child and what he represents. "The Story of the Siren" is structurally like a Chinese box, and the reader is allowed only gradually into its innermost secret: when the priggish narrator drops his notebook on the Deist controversy into the Mediterranean, religion sinks symbolically away and the first lid opens; the second opens when the conventional English tourists leave him alone with the guide; the third, when the guide strips off his clothing and plunges into the water; the fourth, when, in the cave where they are "apart from all the commonplaces that are called reality," where "only the fantastic would be tolerable" (p. 248), the guide tells the narrator the story of his brother and the Siren. "I don't know why," the Englishman says, "but it filled me with desire to help others—the greatest of all our desires, I suppose, and the most fruitless. The desire soon passed" (p. 254). His inadequate response is humanity's answer to the truth, a prelude, however mild, to the climactic murder of the pregnant Maria by a priest. The hope for humanity is killed, the boxes begin to close again, and all that is left is the Sicilian's insistence that: "Silence and loneliness cannot last for ever. It may be a hundred or a thousand years, but the sea lasts longer, and she shall come out of it and sing" (p. 258). The guide's speech is only a pious wish; there is little comfort in it, and even this much is called into doubt as the story ends. As he speaks, the cave symbolically darkens; through its entrance comes the boat of the returning English, the forces of this world, to whom Forster reluctantly gives the victory in this, his last story.

The closest analogue to "The Story of the Siren" is A Passage to India. Only in these two works does Forster acknowledge fully the truth of the Siren's song. But it is clear in The

Eternal Moment as a whole and in *Howards End* that Forster is tending, sometimes unwillingly, in this direction. Between these works and the earlier ones there is not only the difference of mood and atmosphere of which I have spoken; underlying and causing it, there is a difference of perspective. The position from which Forster attacks the prigs, the philistines, and the spectators of "The Celestial Omnibus" or *A Room with a View* is on the whole a secure one. Given his certainty about what the good life is, it is comparatively easy for him to single out its enemies and to satirize them with high spirits. In the later works, though there is no significant change of values, there is increasingly some doubt about the foundations on which they have been built. Forster is, therefore, as much or more concerned after *A Room with a View* with discovering whether there is any order in his universe as he is with combatting the spurious orders men have constructed to keep themselves from facing the truth. The stories in the second collection indicate the direction of Forster's search. It is in the remaining novels, to which we now turn, that the exploration is carried out most fully and with greatest effect.

4 · The Search for Order

1. HOWARDS END

As in *A Room with a View*, so in *Howards End* there is an attempt to "play on the side of Victory," but the later novel has no Lucy and considerably less air and light and view. If optimism achieves a precarious triumph in the world of the Honeychurches and the Emersons, that triumph is still less assured and less believable in the world of the Schlegels, where it is even more obviously desired. *Howards End* is Forster's most ambitious attempt to complete successfully his search for order and harmony, but that attempt is undermined throughout the book by his own doubts and hesitancies. The ambivalence between hope and despair is much more fundamental in *Howards End* than in Forster's other novels, much more deeply ingrained in the very texture of the work. One cannot point merely to the opposition of a Rickie and a Stephen or to a reversal of mood in the final chapter (although that is here too); one must penetrate rather to the not immediately discernible incongruity of the component parts of the book. This internecine struggle is best illustrated by Forster's failure to observe one of his own dicta: in *Aspects of the Novel* he says that "there are in the novel two forces: human beings and a bundle of various things not human beings, and . . . it is the novelist's business to adjust these two forces and conciliate their claims" (p. 99). In *Howards End* the forces are not adjusted, since the book is organized in two different and inharmonious ways: rhetorically, in terms of plot, symbolism, and motif; psychologically, through the dramatization of the search for meaning that Helen and Margaret Schlegel, the leading characters of the novel, pursue. The first way makes use of that "bundle of various things" to project Forster's longing for some ultimate tendency, some assurance of purpose and direction in life as it should be. The second comes closer to his vision of life as it actually is, in all its unpredictable variety and with all its disappointments and failures. That Forster was not conscious of this struggle seems clear, for formal elements tug in one direction, whereas human beings (in their realistic, if not always in their symbolic, roles) tug in another. To understand this dichotomous attitude is to see both why *Howards End* is so complex a book and also why the tensions in it are never satisfactorily resolved.

I

It is the plot of *Howards End* that, most obviously, works in a general way toward the reconciliation of opposed ideas and characters—toward what seems, on its own level, a happy ending. It joins what has been separate and produces an apparent answer to the questions raised in the course of the novel. The plot, in fact, provides what Forster would call "pattern," a shape that is apparent in the several crisscrossings of the paths of the Wilcoxes, the Schlegels, and the Basts, and in the final symbolic coming together of all the characters at Howards End. As we shall see, pattern does not work too well for Forster; [1] he is too dialectical an author, too interested in what cannot be compressed into a neat formula. Somewhat less schematically, the symbolic elements and the predominantly symbolic characters of the book have an effect comparable to the plot's. The most important of this group is Mrs. Wilcox, who has her prototypes in Forster's other novels. She recalls Gino and Stephen Wonham, Stephen's mother and his farmer father, and even Mr. Emerson, but whereas she represents the fullest develop-

---

1 See Chapter VIII of *Aspects of the Novel* for Forster's distinction between pattern and rhythm (the latter, the "internal stitching" of a novel, is also present in *Howards End*). Forster generally finds pattern too mechanical and external to combine well with the richness of life.

ment of certain characteristics all these men and women have in common, she is in some respects less human than any of them. Her symbolic connections are with the land, but she is never sufficiently of the land, of the living earth, to be completely believable. In some ways she is a highly complex person, but even her complexity is static; she already has the answer for which Margaret Schlegel is searching—she *is*, in fact, in all that she represents, that answer. Almost completely pure symbol, Mrs. Wilcox reminds us of a way of life that is passing but that remains for Forster a better, a more significant way.

Mrs. Wilcox, by being herself, is fighting against the twentieth century, against rootlessness, against movement, against the culture of the machine; she is Forster's myth of salvation. To her Forster opposes London, a symbol of all that he hates: flats and flux, indistinction, useless movement, mediocrity, and instability. London makes for separateness: it is against personal relations; it makes individuality almost impossible without money; culture is an alien growth in its barren soil. As the flats and monuments rise and fall, an abyss yawns for the unsuccessful, those who cannot adjust to economic civilization and who are unable to stand upon what Margaret Schlegel calls the "golden islands" of inherited wealth.

A clue to the way of life that Mrs. Wilcox represents, the country life that is contrasted with London, can be discovered in "The Abinger Pageant," one of Forster's two plays. The pageant "tries to show the continuity of country life" (AH, p. 384), and one remark from its epilogue is particularly worth quoting: "*Remember that all this beauty is a gift which you can never replace. . . . You can never, never make the country, because it was made by Time*" (*ibid*., p. 399). The importance of this statement is clear when it is taken in conjunction with one from Forster's other play, "Man made the country as he made the town" (EPL, p. 79). Forster's attitude toward land has ultimately practical meaning. As the visible link between past and present, and as the sign of man's accomplishments and labors, it embodies tradition and allows for steady growth; it preserves somehow the undeniable but inexplicable wisdom of those who live close to the soil. The country is the "natural" order to which Forster turns in so many of his books.

His works contain no reference to nature as God's handiwork, and it is not as a divine emblem that nature is important to him. It is precisely because he doubts the existence of any absolute that he holds as valuable the structures man has been able to forge out of original chaos, and it is because he recognizes how easily all may revert to chaos that he is, for all his liberalism, so cautious and tentative. Man can destroy easily, but it takes him long to build; there is danger in change that is too rapid, too all-embracing, for, as Forster says of the Schlegels' grasping landlord, "he has spilt the precious distillation of the years, and no chemistry of his can give it back again" (p. 158).

It is at Howards End, Mrs. Wilcox's house and the main focus of hope in the novel, that the value of the country and of tradition is most fully symbolized:

[The house] was English and the wych-elm that [Margaret] saw from the window was an English tree. No report had prepared her for its peculiar glory. It was neither warrior, nor lover, nor god; in none of these roles do the English excel. It was a comrade, bending over the house, strength and adventure in its roots, but in its utmost fingers tenderness, and the girth, that a dozen men could not have spanned, became in the end evanescent, till pale bud clusters seemed to float in the air. It was a comrade. House and tree transcended any similes of sex. (pp. 217–18)

That Howards End and the wych-elm somehow represent the England Forster wishes to find, the England that means stability and salvation, is apparent. Both are always identified with the country, and, on one level, as the different characters enter and leave the house, something like a parable of England is being told.[2]

Closely related to Mrs. Wilcox and her house is Miss Avery, a sibylline character whose main function seems to be one of foretelling the return of life to the temporarily uninhabited Howards End. Her interest is in the Howards, of whom Mrs. Wilcox is the last, and not in the Wilcoxes. On first meeting Margaret, she startles her by saying that she took her for

2 See the chapter on *Howards End* in Professor Trilling's *E. M. Forster*. Professor Trilling concerns himself in particular with this aspect of the novel.

the now dead Mrs. Wilcox. The announcement makes it clear that somehow Margaret will be identified with her older friend, since throughout, Miss Avery's role is to make the reader accept the strange events that occur by casting over them a sense of inevitability. Miss Avery, like Mrs. Wilcox, is a symbol pointing to harmony and to the ultimate achievement of that harmony at Howards End.

Even more important than the plot or the symbolism in giving the book an optimistic direction is the thematic motif of "connecting." The prominence that Forster wished to give to this concept is indicated by the fact that the epigraph of the novel is, "Only connect . . . ," but even without so obvious a clue the reader could not fail to be aware of the centrality of the idea of connecting and of its relation to the search for order in the book. Most obviously, Forster is attempting to bring together the ways of life represented by the terms "Wilcoxism" and "Schlegelism." Wilcoxism is the symbol of the outer life, of the life where newspapers and telegrams, motor cars and golf clubs, have the most urgent importance. Wilcoxes appear to be possessed of great strength and determination; they are proven in their ability to control events and people around them. But, as Helen and Margaret Schlegel soon discover, such strength and control tell nothing of the inner man. "Perhaps," Helen comments, "the little thing that says 'I' is missing out of the middle of their heads" (p. 247). In fact, panic and emptiness are the true marks of the Wilcoxes, once their outer shells are pierced and the dark tangle within lies exposed. Moreover, Wilcoxes lack almost completely the sense of self-awareness; they construct for themselves a form, a pattern, a petrified way of life (and in this sense resemble the adherents to the aesthetic view of life) and avoid anything that demands of them personal responses or self-evaluation.

And yet Margaret, at least, who is too honest to deny the good that has been done by men like Henry Wilcox, refuses totally to condemn him or his family. She sees in him the virtues of decision, obedience, and neatness, and she feels that he has grit. Her praise is qualified, but like Forster she feels: "Some day—in the millennium—there may be no need for his type. At present homage is due to it from those who think themselves superior, and who possibly are" (p. 171). Clearly the connection that is sought is not one that will involve a meeting at some mathematical midpoint of Wilcoxism and Schlegelism. Forster and Margaret are aware of the superiority of the Schlegel virtues, and what they desire is a coming together of what is good in both ways of life, not a gross merging of all their respective qualities. The new and better product, it is obvious, will have in it more of Schlegel than of Wilcox.

Schlegelism is somewhat more difficult to define, since Margaret and Helen are more complex and more different from each other than are the Wilcoxes. The description of Wilcoxism has already indicated to some degree what ways of thinking and feeling the sisters hold as most worthwhile. Their allegiance is primarily to the inner life, the life whereby the individual can make direct contact with nature, with art, with whatever is of the spirit in books or places or men. They love most what is direct and personal, whatever is hallowed by tradition and associations, and they care most for their relationships with other human beings. Of course, Margaret and Helen lack something of worldly wisdom. If Henry treats all individuals as representatives of an abstract category, the Schlegel sisters tend to act as if all men could be dealt with on the same level of intelligence and intimacy. They have a certainty about the correctness of their standard just as the Wilcoxes do about theirs; they differ from the Wilcoxes in that theirs involves an appreciation of tolerance and variety and requires constant self-examination.[3]

3 The most interesting example of the failure of the Schlegel method concerns Maragaret's and Helen's brother, Tibby. Tibby, a minor Cecil Vyse, appears rarely in the book, but he is a necessary character. Tibby's attitude toward life partakes both of Schlegelism and Wilcoxism. It is not that he has learned to make the connection that Margaret strives for; rather, he combines much that is bad or inadequate in one and the other. He has neither the Schlegel respect for the inner life nor the Wilcox grit, neither the Wilcox energy nor the Schlegel consciousness. Indeed, though he is a Schlegel by name, Tibby's is not the Schlegel point of view, and the fault is not entirely his: "Just as some people cease to attend when books are mentioned, so Tibby's attention wandered when 'personal relations' came under discussion" (p. 268). The explanation seems to lie in the fact that Tibby has been smothered by his sisters. Helen and, even more, Margaret are strong, dominant, and, to some extent, masculine women, and it is certainly one of Tibby's functions in the book to point up this

It is not only the Wilcox and the Schlegel mentalities that must be brought together, however, or perhaps it can be said that the general connection implies others. " 'Don't brood too much,' [Margaret] wrote to Helen, 'on the superiority of the unseen to the seen. It's true, but to brood on it is medieval. Our business is not to contrast the two, but to reconcile them' " (p. 109). One must reconcile the outer and the inner, the seen and the unseen, business and culture, the monk and the beast in man, the prose and the passion in life. These antitheses appear constantly in the book, and it is Margaret who is the connecting symbol among all these opposed concepts. It is Margaret who defends at least parts of the outer life, who marries Henry Wilcox, who is actual and spiritual heir to Mrs. Wilcox. And Margaret's job is more difficult still than bringing together the best in herself and the best in Henry: she must mediate, too, between Helen's brooding on the unseen and Henry's materialism, between the life with no material security (Leonard Bast's) and the life with nothing but material security (Henry's). She must accommodate her self-awareness to Mrs. Wilcox's intuitive and inarticulate wisdom. She must smooth all the jagged edges of man's world and produce a new and finer harmony, a harmony of man and nature and the unseen.

Howards End differs from the earlier books in that it tries to be more inclusive; what before was held apart is here united (at least on the symbolic level). The inner and the outer, culture and business, country and city are contrasted here not merely to exalt the first of each pair but to join whatever is worthwhile in both. In a way the book seems to be a kind of self-critique: Forster appears to be looking back, indirectly, at his earlier work and finding it wanting in breadth, in charity, in comprehensiveness. The Herritons, the Pembrokes, the Cecils, all find their continuators in the Wilcoxes, but *Howards End* represents a scrupulous attempt to be fair to Wilcoxism, to

---

side of his sisters' characters. Margaret and Helen do, it is true, feel that they lack the Wilcoxian traits of strength, enterprise, and assertiveness, but they lack them only in relation to the "great outer world," not in their own sphere. Tibby remains as a perpetual reminder of the fact that their methods, however good, do not always work, and also of the fact that they can be wrong even in the area of personal relations.

salvage whatever is good in it, to bring at least part of it into the area of grace. So scrupulous did Forster try to be that he evoked the following comment from D. H. Lawrence: "But think you *did* make a nearly deadly mistake glorifying those *business* people in *Howards End*. Business is no good." [4]

But why, it may be asked, are Margaret and Forster so anxious to connect? The answer is not difficult to find, since Forster's earlier novels betray a similar, if not the same, longing. Beneath this desire lies the awareness of "the chaotic nature of our daily lives, and its difference from that orderly sequence that has been fabricated by historians" (p. 112), as well as the recognition of how much of daily life is, once again to use Forster's word, gray. It is this belief that life in itself is nothing, that man must somehow invest it with meaning, that leads Forster to search for a wholeness, a consonance of all forms and levels of existence. A comment from one of Forster's essays may be taken as the final gloss on this aspect of the novel:

> The Saviour of the future—if ever he comes—will not preach a new gospel. He will . . . make effective the good will and the good temper which are already existing. In other words he will introduce a new technique. . . . The desire for it is by no means new. It was expressed, for example, in theological terms by Jacopone da Todi over six hundred years ago. "Ordina questo amore, O tu che m'ami," he said; "O thou who lovest me—set this love in order." . . . Not by becoming better, but by ordering and distributing his native goodness, will Man shut up Force into its box, and so gain time to explore the universe and set his mark upon it worthily. (*TC*, p. 75)

In this paragraph lies the central vision of Forster's novel: earnestly to set in order what is good in the world, to approach what does exist with a new technique, that is Margaret Schlegel's symbolic function, and Forster approves.

But if the book aspires in so many ways to reset the bones of a broken world, to reconcile all extremes in a new order, one must still ask how much is, after all, connected, how successful the synthesis is, and to what extent the hope that Forster here expresses is justified by the book as a whole. To find the contradictory impulse in the novel one must look to the characters

4 Harry T. Moore (ed.), *The Collected Letters of D. H. Lawrence* (New York: The Viking Press, 1962), II, 716.

in the book as they function on a realistic plane, to Helen and Margaret in particular, and observe whether their lives justify the optimism that is expressed by the plot, the symbolism, and the motif of connecting.

II

To one of the characters in *Howards End* " 'the Miss Schlegels' still remained a composite Indian god, whose waving arms and contradictory speeches were the product of a single mind" (p. 148), but it is necessary and important, despite the large number of ideas and ideals they share, to distinguish between the two sisters. Helen is a more dramatic, a less complex, woman than Margaret, for her character and her ideals are more in accord; one can predict on the basis of what she says what Helen will do, and on the basis of what she does what she is likely to say. It is easier to find literary counterparts for Helen than for Margaret, and indeed her feminism, her difficult relations with men, and her penchant for the unseen and the unknown recall at various times Wells's Ann Veronica, Hardy's Sue Bridehead, and Lawrence's Kate Leslie. This is not to say that Forster's Helen is a derivative character or that she lacks individuality; rather, she can be regarded as one embodiment of a type of early twentieth-century woman who made as prominent a place for herself in life as in art. Aware of her new status in a society heretofore dominated by men, eager for, but sometimes apprehensive of, her new privileges and responsibilities, conscious that not all men (or women) regard her with favor, the new woman tends to be somewhat hysterical or extreme, full of proposals and suggestions, eager to espouse schemes, and perhaps equally ready to abandon them. She is between two ages, and her vacillation results in serious upsets of thought and action.

Helen does not, of course, correspond precisely to this composite portrait, but she has much in common with it. Above all, she is attracted by extremes: her actions are precipitous and unplanned, and her thinking inevitably fails to achieve the proportion Margaret praises. Generally Helen's impetuousness, her relentless pursuit of the absolute, is concerned less with the "reality" of the hard and the tangible, which she claims to find in poverty, than with that "reality" which resides in the unseen, whether in the self or in the universe. Characteristically, as she listens to Beethoven's Fifth Symphony, there rises before her a vision in which heroes are suddenly displaced by goblins and in which flaming ramparts crumble at a breath into wretched dust; she is aware of splendor in life but even more of its panic and emptiness, the emptiness and indistinction that are more fundamental than all man's attempts at order.

Helen reaches out naturally toward the ultimate, the pure, the dramatic, and in one respect at least she is much more like her brother than her sister. Helen, too, fails to see life directly, and of course she does not see it whole. She reminds the reader perhaps less of Cecil Vyse than of Rickie Elliot, for her basic impulses are good, thwarted though they are by the extremism of her character. She is more passionate than her brother, more sympathetic, more adaptable, and unlike him she is capable of change; but she shares with Tibby the proclivity to conceive life in terms of art (though her imagination is more fantastic and pictorial than his) and the inability, on the whole, to establish good personal relations (though, unlike him, she does value and desire them). Helen illustrates, in many ways better than Margaret herself, Margaret's dictum that one must first make excursions into the realms of the extreme before attaining to proportion. Helen is volatile and unpredictable, her actions have a frenetic quality about them, but she does come to have self-awareness and she does try to make herself a better person. Consequently she is sympathetically drawn by Forster, and the reader is invited to view her quests in search of the absolute with a critical but friendly eye.

Both Helen's failures and her changing attitude can be best observed in terms of her relations with men, for it is in these relations that her basic inability to connect with other people is clearest. "The sisters," Forster comments, "were alike as little girls, but at the time of the Wilcox episode their methods were beginning to diverge; the younger [Helen] was apt to entice people, and, in enticing them, to be herself enticed; the elder went straight ahead, and accepted an occasional failure as part of the game" (p. 32). The "Wilcox episode" refers to Helen's

brief romantic interest in Paul Wilcox, though it is more accurate to say that, through its most tangible and eligible representative, Helen falls in love with the idea of Wilcoxism itself.
Feminist though she is (or possibly for that very reason), Helen
is overwhelmed and pleased by her first encounter with active,
practical men who make nonsense of all her ideas and ideals,
not by reasoning with her, but by flatly and gruffly telling her
that she is talking rubbish. Surrounded by motor cars and cigar
smoke, she happily watches her intellectual edifices crumble,
and that night, in the garden of Howards End, she falls in love
and is kissed. The next morning, when she sees Paul, she realizes that he no longer loves her, indeed that he never loved her
at all, and again, but more firmly and absolutely this time, she
espouses the Schlegel values and ideals. Henceforth the inner
life is for her not primary or part of a larger synthesis, but all
in all; Wilcoxism becomes associated with Beethoven's goblins,
and she turns against everything it represents; there are panic
and emptiness on the one side, personal relations on the other,
and she has no interest in the accommodation of the two.

Filled with hate, Helen is now less, rather than more, successful in her relations with others. There is no room in her for
love, only for devotion to causes, and the causes she chooses are
those in which the opposition between the good and Wilcoxism
can be made complete. The effects of her brief relationship
with Paul continue to echo in her bitter mind and lead directly
to her brief affair with Leonard Bast, the lower-middle-class
young man who is taken up by the Schlegels and who comes to
represent for them a goblin footfall "risen out of the abyss . . .
telling of a life where love and hatred had both decayed" (p.
121). Leonard is a symbol for Helen, a symbol of all that is not
Wilcoxian: he is poor, he is striving after culture as best he
can, he is, in his economic capacity, one of the organized, not
one of the organizers, and he has a highly developed sense of
personal responsibility. He is indeed, at first meeting, attractive
to both Helen and Margaret, but as Margaret builds up a relationship with Henry Wilcox (and probably, in Helen's eyes,
joins forces with him), Helen moves closer to Leonard. When
Leonard loses his job because (indirectly) of Henry and when
Helen learns that his "wife" had been Henry's mistress, the

character of their relationship changes. "Helen loved the absolute. Leonard had been ruined absolutely, and had appeared to her as a man apart, isolated from the world" (p. 334). For a brief moment Helen and Leonard come together; there is no love, but on Leonard's part a desire to please and perhaps a need to forget his despair, and on Helen's, the wish to know the ultimate, in whatever form.

Helen leaves the next day for the continent, and it is not until Margaret sees her again at Howards End that she realizes her sister is pregnant. What is not so immediately apparent is that Helen has profited from her eight months away, that she has managed to come to terms with her hatred at last. Helen does grow and mature, and it can be said that she finally achieves a kind of proportion. If she is not an altogether complete woman, if she is incapable of significant relations with men, still she comes at the last to recognize her limitations. Helen's search for meaning helps her to attain to self-knowledge and allows her, if not to love all men, at least to subdue her hatred to tolerance and understanding. Still, the maturity and wisdom that Helen wins are hardly commensurate with the hope expressed by the other elements of the novel, and one must look to Margaret to see whether the hope is ever justified or whether it is, after all, incapable of realization in the world as Forster sees it.

Margaret is clearly the more aware, the more stable, of the two sisters. She is, Forster has said, one of the characters he enjoys thinking about,[5] and indeed, even when one has admitted all her faults—a slight masculinity, the blue-stocking quality to which her practicality sometimes gives rise, the occasional tendency to go too far in praising actions without regarding their consequences, her capacity for making mistakes—still one is bound to consider her a remarkable and admirable woman. She proceeds quietly and carefully to do whatever she considers to be right, to bring about, in herself or others, whatever changes she feels to be necessary, and she acts in this way even though it is less easy for her to do so than it is for Helen. Margaret, unlike her sister, refuses to follow the path of least

5 Furbank and Haskell, p. 33.

resistance, the path that follows the curve of the emotions and the desires. For Margaret there is a distinction between that which is most congenial and that which is, in her estimation, correct; she tries, in so far as she can, to do justice to the latter. Margaret, no less than Helen, is attracted by the inner life, and, by nature, she is a lover of moderation; still she attempts to connect the inner with the outer and to achieve a balance by coming to know the partial truths that lie to the far sides of truth itself. It is not easy for her to be extreme, and therefore there is a marked contrast between her character and her ideals, but she does make the effort to see life fully and whole.

Underlying Margaret's belief that life must be given order and meaning there exists, perhaps, not only the consciousness of the chaotic nature of twentieth-century society, but also the perception of the chaotic nature of life itself. And although her search for significance leads her at times to speculate on another world or worlds, her eyes are generally directed to the world around her; her desire, in the last analysis, is for hope on this side of the grave. Indeed Margaret's whole philosophy is predicated on a belief in the value and interest of individual men; her beliefs, her values, her ideals, all are man-centered; the unseen, in and around man, is to be approached through man and to be conceived in terms of him.

Naturally enough, then, the most crucial event in Margaret's life involves a personal relationship. Her marriage to Henry Wilcox is her most optimistic, but also her most disappointing, venture into the world that is not naturally her own. Something has already been indicated about Henry in the description of Wilcoxism—his in part superficial masculinity, his inability to react personally to people or things, the defenses that keep him from contact with the world—but it is in his relations with Margaret that he most completely reveals himself. It is not long before she discovers that "it was hard going in the roads of Mr. Wilcox's soul. . . . Outwardly he was cheerful, reliable, and brave; but within, all had reverted to chaos, ruled, so far as it was ruled at all, by an incomplete asceticism" (p. 197). This description of Henry inevitably recalls comparable characters in others of Forster's novels. The inner chaos beneath the rigid exterior, the asceticism, the fear of passion, and the false sense of religion link him with the villains of *A Room with a View.* "Unchastity and infidelity," Forster comments, "were as confused to him as to the Middle Ages, his only moral teacher" (p. 273). The blight of the incomplete man is on Henry, and although he does not, as did his prototypes, mold reality into an artistic form, he nevertheless imposes on it a rigid and false order of his own. His mind works naturally in stereotypes and clichés, categorizing men and women rather than responding to them, and his world is inevitably a lonely one, for it is populated not by individuals but by types.

Henry, of course, has needs and desires, and in his own way falls in love with Margaret. His proposal is explicable enough, but it is more difficult to understand why Margaret marries him. Why do the scales not fall from her eyes as they did from Lucy Honeychurch's? Margaret does seem to enter into the relationship with full awareness of what is involved: asked by Helen immediately after the proposal whether she loves Henry, she answers that she does not but that she will, and Forster remarks that "if insight were sufficient, if the inner life were the whole of life, their happiness had been assured" (p. 194). So Margaret does seem to know Henry, but does she fully understand the implications of her knowledge? One wonders if she is able to envision the man who is the sum total of all the qualities she recognizes and if that man is, as she thinks, "a real man." In part Forster seems to be trying to show that Margaret is as yet somewhat naïve, that she does not fully realize what she is saying when she speaks of her love as prose. Also, it begins to appear likely that Margaret's love results, at least in part, from her longing to be fair to a way of living opposite to her own, to connect the life of personal relations, which she cherishes, with the outer life and the grit that are Henry's. It is possible both not to sneer at Wilcoxes and not to love them, but it is perhaps not possible for Margaret, in whom the intellectual desire and the emotional need to reconcile are so strong.

Certainly, however clear Margaret's vision may be, it is based on the assumption that Henry will change, that "mature as he was, she might yet be able to help him to the building of the rainbow bridge that should connect the prose in us with the passion" (p. 196). But even before her marriage Margaret is forced to become more conscious of the difficulties implicit in any attempt to make Henry a different sort of person. "There was one quality in Henry," Forster notes, "for which she was never prepared, however much she reminded herself of it: his obtuseness. He simply did not notice things, and there was no more to be said" (p. 197). Henry's obtuseness is particularly marked in the way he confronts the evidence of his affair with Jacky Bast. Margaret feels her love almost stifled, but Henry, after a shoddy explanation, begins immediately to rebuild his defenses, and Forster gives another reason for Margaret's love when he says: "Pity was at the bottom of her actions all through this crisis. Pity, if one may generalize, is at the bottom of woman. When men like us, it is for our better qualities . . . but unworthiness stimulates woman" (p. 257).

So Margaret does marry Henry, and although the marriage—or, at any rate, Henry—seems to some degree unworthy of her, her action is explicable in terms of her personality. Moved by pity and unworthiness, anxious both to appreciate and to improve Henry (and indeed all Wilcoxes), still perhaps overly idealistic, surely too eager to see other points of view than her own and to do justice to them, influenced in the end by her desire for order and for proportion and by her feeling that these are to be achieved only by doing some violence to her own impulses and wishes, Margaret is, after all, genuinely in love; and one wonders only whether that love can persist, whether Margaret, once married, will deepen her critical awareness and thus inevitably tip the scales in favor of truth.

Exactly that happens, and Helen proves to be the rock on which the marriage vessel founders. Back at Howards End for one day, Helen, whom Margaret and Henry now know to be pregnant, asks her sister to spend the evening with her at the house. Henry refuses permission because, he intimates, he does not wish his house defiled by the presence of a woman bearing an illegitimate child. Margaret begins to allude to Henry's own sexual lapse, while Henry, unwilling to face himself, assumes an increasingly arrogant moral position and tone. At last Margaret is unable to contain herself any longer: " 'Not any more of this!' she cried. 'You shall see the connection if it kills you, Henry!'" (p. 325). Henry, of course, will not make the connection; indeed he accuses his wife of blackmail, and she leaves him to return to Helen, having, in effect, renounced all hope of making Henry a better person and having refused any longer to accept him as he is.

That evening she is drawn still more to her sister and to the Schlegel point of view: the outer life appears less substantial; the inner, closer to the truth. The next morning confirms all her feelings. Henry sends his son to investigate the situation at Howards End; there Charles comes upon Leonard Bast and, intending to thrash him, inadvertently kills the father of Helen's child. Leonard's death has later, but at present unforeseen, effects, and for the moment Margaret refuses to let it influence her decision to leave Henry. Pity remains and perhaps the shadow of her former feeling, but she has progressed beyond her husband, even beyond her former self, and she is unable any longer to believe in the possibility of a successful relationship with him.

On the whole the development in Margaret is, and Forster seems to regard it as, a good one. Surer of herself and of her ideas, she becomes a more solid and stable person, creative in a new way, able to find new significance in life. And it is this new Margaret who is able to see in Leonard's death a meaning she has till now been able to apprehend only dimly:

Here Leonard lay dead in the garden, from natural causes; yet life was a deep, deep river, death a blue sky, life was a house, death a wisp of hay, a flower, a tower, life and death were anything and everything, except this ordered insanity, where the king takes the queen and the ace the king. Ah, no; there was beauty and adventure behind, such as the man at her feet had yearned for; there was hope this side of the grave; there were truer relationships beyond the limits that fetter us now. As a prisoner looks up and sees stars beckoning, so she, from the turmoil and horror of those days, caught glimpses of the diviner wheels. . . . To what ultimate harmony we tend she did not know, but there seemed great chance that a child would be born into the world, to take the great chances of beauty and adventure that the world offers. . . . Here was the father; leave it at that. Let Squalor be turned into Tragedy, whose eyes are the stars, and whose hands hold the sunset and the dawn. (pp. 348–49)

Standing at Leonard's feet, Margaret is saved; Leonard, dead from "natural causes," is a sign of the unnaturalness, the unreality of the lives she and all the others have been leading. Suddenly she is able to see the pettiness of their actions, the loss of their true selves, and her new knowledge enables her to glimpse the poetry at the heart of things, the adventure and the beauty the world offers. Like Mr. Lucas in the tree at Colonus, Margaret has a sudden revelation of the possibilities of life. In the beautiful riot of images that expresses her vision, one can watch her mind moving easily back and forth between the ideas of death and life. The wisp of hay and the house, the two chief redemptive symbols of the novel, are associated, respectively, with death and life; death is a flower, while life is a river, symbol heretofore of all that is unstable. Confronted by death, Margaret transcends the ordered insanity that has been her life for the past days and sees life enhanced by death, new life arising from the dead ashes.

But something prevents the vision from seeming perfect. That Margaret is better able to appreciate both the good and the bad in life, that she can see life whole as never before, that she knows now how to distinguish between what is important and what is mean or petty, all of this is obvious. And yet one knows how severely Margaret's hopes in Henry, in the outer life in general, have been constricted, how much less reason she has to be optimistic about the possibility of connecting. How does she bring her intuition of life's potential to bear on her knowledge of life's disappointments? She does so in a way that is characteristic of many Forsterian heroes and heroines: possibility and hope are once again projected into the future; it is Helen's child who will be able to take advantage of the beauty and adventure in the world. There is no mention of how Margaret herself will act; one feels somehow that her day is over, that she herself feels this. If she emerges from the battle purer, she is nonetheless scarred, victorious but subdued. Death suggests life, but it is life in the future, life for the generations to come.

Had the book closed at this point, the reader would have felt some pity, more admiration, for Margaret, and the novel would have had completeness, would, perhaps, have been even more satisfying. It would then have recorded the tragedy of an honest but unsuccessful attempt to achieve a desirable connection, an order, in a world essentially hostile to such efforts. Life has left its mark on Margaret, but she has been equal, or almost equal to it. One can imagine her, parted from Henry, building for herself a richer, if sadder, life. But the story is not over; the last pages record Forster's final attempt to adjust and conciliate what he calls the two forces in the novel.

Howards End begins to take a new turn when Mr. Wilcox asks to see Margaret and tells her that the verdict at the inquest of Leonard's death will be manslaughter and that, as a result, Charles may go to jail. "I don't know what to do— what to do," Henry says. " 'I'm broken—I'm ended.' No sudden warmth arose in her. She did not see that to break him was her only hope. . . . She did what seemed easiest—she took him down to recruit at Howards End" (p. 353). One cannot help feeling at this point that the demands of the plot are becoming too insistent and that behind the plot is an author who is not altogether willing to allow his characters to follow their own paths of development. It is, after all, only a series of fortuitous circumstances, highly unlikely ones, that brings Margaret and Henry together again: the coincidence of the arrival of Leonard and Charles at Howards End when Margaret and Helen are staying there, the accidental death of Leonard, and the (largely) unjustified conviction of Charles. It is as if Forster, no less than Margaret, were intent on connecting above all, on achieving order, on forcing the fusion of disparate things and people.

In any case, the last chapter creates a strange dual effect. On the symbolic level a great resolution is effected: Schlegels and Wilcoxes come together at Howards End; Margaret at last achieves the reconciliation of the outer and the inner life by bringing together her sister and her husband; and Henry, willing Howards End to Margaret, implements his first wife's bequest—and the property, destined next for Margaret's nephew, is to continue into the future. England past and future, upper and lower classes, all meet and merge in the house and beside the tree that symbolizes the comradeship that is England's greatest gift.

The harmony that is apparent at Howards End is less obvious, however, on the realistic level, on the level where the characters are themselves rather than vehicles of larger and more abstract concepts. Above all, Margaret makes the greatest personal sacrifice in her role of symbolic connector. To begin with, one cannot quite believe in her return to Henry. She realizes herself the impossibility of a significant relationship between them, and if her caring for him in his moment of crisis is understandable, still when, as the last chapter opens, it is indicated that Margaret will henceforth remain at Howards End with her husband, the reader inevitably experiences a feeling of disappointment. Margaret knows (as we do) that Henry is not worthy of her, and it seems a forfeit either of her principles or of herself to re-establish a connection that cannot be. If her only hope is "to break him," then the inadequacy of the relationship is to a large degree presupposed.

And Margaret disappoints in other ways as well. It is her symbolic function also to effect a *rapprochement* with Mrs. Wilcox, to come closer to the instinctive and quiet wisdom of her older friend. This she does throughout the book, and in large measure the change is a good one. Margaret becomes less frenetic, less like her Bohemian friends; as the sense of flux all around her is moderated, as she relies less on the excitement of new movements and ideas, her stature as an individual grows. But in her final phase Margaret betrays the very proportion she holds as an ideal: love of stability turns into love of comfort; concern for order becomes concern for neatness; desire for significance leads to desire for busyness. An anti-intellectual Margaret is a poor substitute for Miss Schlegel of Wickham Place; she is, after all, fascinating precisely because of her intelligence, her awareness, her conscious approach to life. To watch her transfiguration into another Mrs. Wilcox, herself a not completely adequate character, is to perceive a certain loss and waste. What, one wonders, has happened to her revelation of adventure and beauty? Add the fact that Margaret admits to an inability to love children, and the final picture of her is somewhat barren, even pitiable. Connection, such as it is, is purchased at the expense of vitality, and it is a lesser Margaret who sits quietly sewing near the shadow of Howards End, a Margaret whose aim is no longer a search for harmony, but a sewing of things together, a patching and binding of worn and wasted lives.

The other characters of the novel, on the nonsymbolic level, are no more satisfactory than Margaret. Helen admits that she is forgetting Leonard, indeed that love has never been, and will never be, the great thing in her life. She is better able to understand Henry, even to see why Margaret married him, and to that extent she is more tolerant and understanding, but there is something vacuous about her life, too, as it stretches into the future. From Helen, even more than from Margaret, one expects tremendous vitality and joy in living, but it is apparently to be her fate to share in the quiescent country life of her sister and her brother-in-law. Helen's extremism has been too thoroughly curtailed, leaving her, like her sister, less than, as well as different from, what she was.

Leonard Bast, of course, is dead. " 'Yes, yes,' " Helen says to Margaret " 'but what has Leonard got out of life?' 'Perhaps an adventure.' 'Is that enough?' 'Not for us. But for him.' " (p. 357).[6] But still Leonard is dead, and one wonders whether an adventure was enough to justify his life. A life of economic and psychological suffering cannot be that easily written off as good or worthwhile. Ironically, he is killed by the Schlegel sword, the sword that had been sheathed by Margaret and Helen's father because of his dislike of violence, and though it is wielded by a Wilcox, it is true nonetheless that Leonard dies through the Schlegel sisters. To the last Leonard blames himself, not Helen, for their relationship; he becomes subject to the horror of continual remorse. Leonard, Forster says, "was driven straight through its torments and emerged pure, but enfeebled—a better man, who would never lose control of himself again, but also a smaller man, who had less to control" (p. 334). Better but smaller: those words seem to describe most of the characters in the book; they are robbed of tragedy, of stature, almost of will and desire.

The Wilcoxes too seem to undergo worse fortunes without becoming better people. Charles is in jail; his wife, her life

6 Margaret's statement is curious, for it is she who had seen, at Leonard's death, the possibility of beauty and adventure in life.

smashed, is only more pathetic than ever; and Henry Wilcox, it must be admitted, is no closer to connecting than before his collapse. Mr. Wilcox is, in his fashion, happy at Howards End, happy with his wife, happy even with Helen and her son. Superficially it can be said that he has managed at last to enter into relationships successfully (and symbolically, of course, the connection is made), but the truth is that Henry makes contact by submission, not connection. "The male is too thoroughly gelded," [7] Professor Trilling has said, and Margaret herself feels that "there was something uncanny in her triumph. She, who had never expected to conquer anyone, had charged straight through these Wilcoxes and broken up their lives" (pp. 360–61).

It must be acknowledged that the effect Margaret and Helen have on others is more destructive than regenerative. The worlds of business and of culture are, after all, not united; satisfactory personal relationships are not, with one exception, brought about. The list of incomplete or imperfect relationships—Helen and Paul, Helen and Leonard, Margaret and Henry, Mr. Wilcox and Mrs. Wilcox, Leonard and his wife—bulks much larger than the relationship between Margaret and Helen, where true comradeship is achieved. Communication is minimal in the book: Mrs. Wilcox does manage, in some ineffable way, to communicate with Margaret, and Margaret and Helen do understand each other, but generally the barriers are too high or too thick.

Still, it must be remembered that, although Margaret and Helen break up the lives of those with whom they come into contact, the fault is not ultimately theirs. It is because the Wilcoxes so stubbornly refuse to connect, refuse to treat people as human beings, because Leonard, through no fault of his own, is so situated economically as to be unable to assimilate the Schlegel ideals of culture and the inner life; it is for these reasons that their lives fail. Margaret and Helen can hardly be blamed for being better people, indeed can hardly be blamed for trying to make others better. Their fault is, at the last, that they are not themselves bigger people, that they do not fully

7 Trilling, E. M. Forster, p. 135.

justify through their own example the destruction which they, with all good intentions, bring about. The difficulty lies, perhaps, in the fact that the last chapter represents not Margaret's search for meaning, but Forster's (in a sense different from that in which the whole book is Forster's search), and that two impulses are straining him in opposite directions.

That there are two tendencies throughout the book has already been noted, but it is in the final chapter that their incompatibility becomes most apparent. The conflicts between optimism and pessimism, between hope and belief are most marked here. It is not only that, while formal resolution is most complete, Margaret and Helen are, for the first time in the novel, less satisfactory than one would want or expect them to be; there are other indications as well. Most clearly there is the reappearance of the theme that figured in the earlier novels, the theme of continuance of life. In *Howards End* it is in connection with Mrs. Wilcox and her influence on Margaret (spiritual continuation) that the theme is most elaborately worked out, but it receives its most obvious treatment in the last chapter. There a link is established not only between the first and second Mrs. Wilcox, but between Margaret and her young nephew, the child of Helen and Leonard. The link is Howards End itself, which Henry leaves to his wife and, after her, to Helen's baby. The past meets the future in the present, and the continuance of the generations is assured.

Symbolically, Margaret's nephew is the most unifying figure in the novel. His life and his inheritance are due, in different ways, to Margaret, to Helen, to Henry, to Leonard, and to Mrs. Wilcox; but again, he is, like the redemptive children in the earlier novels, necessarily the least developed character in the book. One cannot help feeling once more that hope is embodied in a child because the belief in that hope is actually so tentative, so insecure. Helen's son is the future, and one cannot deny a future that has about it so few definite and tangible marks or signs. A nameless innocence, the child promises a better world than his elders have been able to construct; he is the living and vital presence among broken and resigned adults, the new life, and in Forster's world, the familiar life, that arises from death. Playing in the field, he is connected with

hay and sun and flowers, with a fertility and promise that Schlegels, as well as Wilcoxes, have lost. The whole formal structure
of the novel points to the boy at the end, the boy who, like so
many of his brothers in the tales, is the symbol of the unsoiled,
primitive imagination. If one forgets for the moment the Wilcoxes gathered in the dark house and Margaret and Helen sitting on the lawn, it is possible to imagine the new age soon to
come.

But behind the playing child the Schlegel sisters are dis-
cussing with greater awareness the possibility of a better future.
"There are moments," Margaret says, "when I feel Howards
End peculiarily our own."

"All the same, London's creeping."
[Helen] pointed over the meadow—over eight or nine meadows,
but at the end of them was a red rust. . . .
Margaret knew that her sister spoke truly. Howards End, Oniton,
the Purbeck Downs, the Oderberge, were all survivals, and the
melting-pot was being prepared for them. Logically, they had no
right to be alive. One's hope was in the weakness of logic. Were
they possibly the earth beating time? (pp. 358–59)

One's hope was in the weakness of logic. In those words lies
the key to the conflict of moods in the last chapter. It is apparent that London threatens, that the world will be all gray;
both Margaret and Helen recognize the dominant tendency of
their civilization. But they refuse to believe what they see. Still
their hope is not sufficiently sure or triumphant (nor is Forster's) to make the possibility of another future convincing.
Something about their talk, about their actions even, belies
that possibility. The chapter expresses hope, but somehow conveys sadness, and the last words are after all too ecstatic for
what has gone before: " 'The field's cut!' Helen cried excit-
edly—'the big meadow! We've seen to the very end, and it'll be
such a crop of hay as never!' " (p. 362). There is a note of
forced joy in Helen's exclamations, too much enthusiasm, too
much ardor for a future that is not, as it seems, a bright or
promising one. The reader cannot but be aware of London
washing towards the shores of the island that is Howards End
and, however sadly, recognize that it will be engulfed by the
monotonously moving waves.

This conflict, so apparent at the end, is, after all, latent in the whole book, although there it appears most obviously in the defective articulation of the symbolic and realistic levels. In effect, Forster achieves at the last, not proportion, but the halfway meeting of opposites that Margaret deplores. Something has not been said or acknowledged, and therefore the solution is, at the best, unsteady, at the worst, facile. The best criticism of the novel is Forster's own: proportion must come at the end, not at the beginning, and Forster is not yet at the end of his search. Seen as the predecessor of A *Passage to India*, the book can be considered the last of Forster's efforts to keep himiself from yielding to a bitter and deeply pessimistic view of the universe; hope and despair are still at war with each other, and the battle is largely inconclusive. If hope, at the last, seems victorious, it has achieved at the best a Pyrrhic victory; the fight will begin again in Forster's last novel, and the uneasy truce is apparent even now.

2. A PASSAGE TO INDIA

The gulf that separates A *Passage to India* from Forster's earlier novels is far more profound than that which exists between any two others of his books; the gulf is not unbridgeable, but its presence must be acknowledged if the book is to be understood. To be sure, A *Passage to India* may be regarded as presenting the final resolution of the various attempts at a consistent attitude toward the world expressed in the four previous books, and in this sense the novel appears to be the culmination of a steady, if arduous, development. Still, the book differs in kind, as well as in degree, from its predecessors; it is, as almost all readers agree, Forster's most artistically satisfying and philosophically profound novel, and it has about it a sureness that all of the earlier books in some degree lack. Writing to Forster about A *Passage to India*, G. Lowes Dickinson commented: "Whereas in your other books your kind of double vision squints—this world, and a world or worlds behind—here it all comes together" (*GLD*, p. 216). It comes together because Forster manages finally to accept fully the pessimistic implications of his way of regarding life, and he is able therefore to produce

a world that has both artistic and intellectual integrity. Forster's experiences during the fourteen years preceding 1924—
in the war, in India, in Egypt—seem to have crystallized his
discontents and to have led him to a reassessment of men and
the world. His last novel substitutes for the primitivism of the
English Stephen or the Italian Gino the primal quality of India
itself. For the first time Forster looks beneath all structures, beneath all man's efforts at civilization, and attempts to see unambiguously what, if anything, was in the beginning.

I

The early pages of Part I, "Mosque," are concerned primarily with showing the relations between the British and the
Indians, the rulers and the ruled. The British as a class are the
more easily typified, and their chief characteristics are revealed
in Forster's description of the civil station of Chandrapore, the
home and symbol of the determined but uneasy foreign rule:
cold, sensible, colorless, the civil station is, like the British, lacking in imagination, lacking in sympathy. The most significant
element in the description is that which relates to the disposi-
tion of the roads of the civil station. The intersecting right
angles at which they meet symbolize the imposed, the intellectual, the unnatural order that the British have manufactured
in India, an order that can exist only by ignoring or suppressing
all the untidiness of those elements of life that do not conform
to the pattern. The little pockets of civilization the Anglo-
Indians have established are a tribute to their energy and to
their determination, but not to their feelings or understanding,
and consequently they remain isolated in the vastness of the
India with which they have no real contact. The order of the
civil station, as the book tries to show, is spurious, analogous to
those created by Forster's characters from Philip Herriton to
Henry Wilcox—ultimately it cannot last, cannot exist at all.

India in general and the native section of Chandrapore in
particular stand in direct opposition to the tidy, well-ordered
British community. Chandrapore is a sprawling growth from the
Indian soil; its monotony is the monotony of the mud that surrounds the city; it is indeed almost part of the soil, of the river,

of the tropical vegetation. Its outlines are indistinct, blurred, amorphous, and whatever order it has is almost that of the natural world. One of the lessons that newly arrived English must learn is that there is no privacy in India, no sharp boundaries, no clear distinctions between men and animals or between men and nature: men may seem like mud moving, the town an amoebalike creature; everything fuses and changes; reality melts away into appearance, appearance becomes suddenly substantial. India is kaleidoscopic; it has all the variety of Nature, all its transmutations, all its inconsistencies; everything seems and nothing is; to each person and from every view the scene is different. Only one thing is certain: the strength of the nonhuman world. Beside the trees and the animals, man and his words are small and insignificant; man cannot understand that to which he gives names, for it is greater than he is, and his control is ultimately illusory. Whatever order there may be is too immense for man to comprehend, if indeed there is any order at all.

It is because the British do not understand the true nature of India that their rule is so unsuccessful, their contact with the Indians so limited and meaningless. Looking at the intersecting roads of the civil station, one of the Indians in the novel feels them to be "symbolic of the net Great Britain had thrown over India" (p. 18). The British raj is an order of force and will, not of love and understanding. What is needed, says one of the characters in the book, is "good will and more good will and more good will" (p. 55), and, in so far as A *Passage to India* is a political novel (which it is only partly and secondarily), these words constitute Forster's answer to the problem of British rule.[1]

Against the background of British-Indian distrust and hatred, smaller and more personal dramas are played out, and although the atmosphere of discord and misunderstanding is

---

1 Compare this passage taken from Forster's last letter written from India and included in *The Hill of Devi*: "*I have been with pro-government and pro-English Indians all this time, so cannot realize the feeling of the other party: and am only sure of this—that we were paying for the insolence of Englishmen and Englishwomen out here in the past. I don't mean that good manners can avert a political upheaval. But they can minimise it, and come nearer to averting it in the East than elsewhere*" (p. 237).

apparent from the beginning, Part I seems, at least on the surface, to be devoted in large measure to attempts on the part of the major characters to establish ties of friendship and confidence. It is the cool season,[2] and the focus of the opening sections is on two Englishwomen who, having just arrived in India, are totally free of any prejudice and on a group of Mohammedans who, embittered though they are by their treatment at the hands of the British, are still more able to comprehend and to be comprehended by sympathetic Westerners than are their fellow Indians, the Hindus. The time for sympathy and kindness is not yet past, and the conditions are propitious, at least for a while.

The first and the most important of the meetings that take place in the novel is that between Mrs. Moore and Dr. Aziz. Aziz, a young Mohammedan, is the human embodiment of all that is symbolized by the "mosque," which serves as the title of the first part and in which the meeting takes place. The dualism that attracts him in the play of black and white on the front of the mosque finds its counterpart in his own character, as does the contention of shadows within the building. For Aziz the affective life is the real and important one, but though his loves are strong and immediate, their objects are often, at least in part, unreal. What is steady in him is the desire to find beauty and the desire to love and be loved, but his life "though vivid was largely a dream" (p. 70). He is in many ways confused and disordered, overemotional and too sensitive, but, unlike the ruling British, he comes close to the ideal of what Forster calls the developed heart. However great the element of fantasy in his life, he is sure of the holiness of the heart's affections.

It is significant that Aziz is first attracted by Mrs. Moore's voice, for voices are important to Forster; they betray personality, and Mrs. Moore's youthful voice announces her spirit. She is still in the early stages of her "passage to India," and is filled with the Whitmanian ardor and optimism to which the title

---

2 In his notes to the "Everyman" edition of his novel, Forster says that "the three sections into which [the book] is divided, Mosque, Caves, Temple, also represent the three seasons of the Cold Weather, the Hot Weather, and the Rains, which divide the Indian year" (p. xxxi).

of the book probably refers.[3] In India as companion to Adela Quested, who has come to see whether she wishes to marry Mrs. Moore's son Ronny, she is filled with a great love and excitement for everything around her. For Mrs. Moore, God is everywhere, and affection accepts no artificial boundaries; her religious and her personal sympathies have a universality that sets them off sharply from the prevalent attitudes of the Anglo-Indian community, whose God and whose personal relations are both severely limited and insular. Mrs. Moore is, as Aziz tells her, Oriental as well as Western, and her God is as at home in a mosque as in a church.

The meeting between Aziz and Mrs. Moore is the crucial incident of the first part of the book, representing, as it does, the coming together, through "the secret understanding of the heart," of two widely different human beings. Communication is established and the encounter has important and lasting effects for both the young Mohammedan and the elderly woman. For Aziz, Mrs. Moore is a friend, one whom he can love without any further thought; for Mrs. Moore, Aziz is a charming young man who somehow represents the goodness and meaning she wishes to find in India, as in the universe, and whose absence she has already begun to feel in the Anglo-Indians. After she has left him, "a sudden sense of unity, of kinship with the heavenly bodies, passed into the old woman and out, like water through a tank, leaving a strange freshness behind" (p. 32). The possibility of human affection has been established and remains, however weakly, as a hopeful theme in the generally harsh and bleak symphony of the novel.

The other important relationship that develops in the first part of the novel is that between Aziz and the English schoolmaster, Cyril Fielding. Fielding, who seems much like Forster, is rational, tolerant, sympathetic, and independent; like Forster, he loves Italy and is interested in individuals. He is regarded with suspicion by the men, and particularly by the women, of the civil station, and, forced against his will to choose between Indians and English, he reluctantly makes the

3 See the article by Paul Fussell, Jr., "E. M. Forster's Mrs. Moore: Some Suggestions," *Philological Quarterly*, XXXII (October, 1953), 391, where Forster's changing views of Walt Whitman are traced.

decision in favor of Indians and remains on uneasy terms with
the world of the club. Aziz is immediately attracted by the fact
that he finds in Fielding's house "some luxury . . . but no
order—nothing to intimidate poor Indians" (p. 67), and Fielding returns the affection with equal speed if not with equal
emotion. As in the meeting between Aziz and Mrs. Moore, so
here, communication is achieved largely as the result of nonverbal, unarticulated factors. Something above or beyond words
brings each of the pairs together and forges a link in each case.
The situations are not, however, identical, for in an important sense Mrs. Moore and Aziz are far more like one another than either is like Fielding. The Englishman is not only
more rational, but more self-conscious, than the other two. To
a small but important extent he has in him something of the
same thing that made Philip Herriton or Cecil Vyse ineffective.
His virtues, and they are many, entail his defects, and his ra-
tionality leads to limitation as well as to clarity. So his friendship with Aziz is genuine but somehow restricted; he can,
perhaps, give all his love, but not all of himself, and even as
the two men begin their friendship, some uneasiness seems to
encircle it.

That uneasiness is made manifest at the tea party to which
the meeting between Aziz and Fielding is merely the prelude.
There is every reason to expect the party to be a success, and
one anticipates that at this gathering further barriers to communication will be broken down. And yet everything goes
wrong. It becomes clear that the symbolism of the word
"mosque" is double, that if, on the one hand, it implies the possibility of communication, still, "in every instance this larger
meaning always implies its opposite or near opposite, an ambivalence finely suggested by the first description of the
mosque." [4] The whole scene at Fielding's house is shot through
with irony, a sad irony in a way, for this largest effort yet at
coming together ends, ultimately, in complete failure and makes
clear how unstable is the order that at first seems possible.

4 Reuben A. Brower, *The Fields of Light* (New York: Oxford
University Press, 1951), p. 185. I am much indebted to Professor Brower's
entire chapter on Forster in this book, as will be apparent in my discussions of the major symbols of the novel.

The party, which begins auspiciously, soon becomes strange and strained when Adela Quested remarks that she hates mysteries. Mrs. Moore answers that she likes mysteries but dislikes muddles, and Fielding joins in by saying that they are the same. All the implications of the conversation are not immediately apparent, but it is an important one, for it says something both of the speakers and of the themes of the book. Adela shares Fielding's rational attitude toward the universe—is, indeed, a good deal more limited and dry in her approach—and it is not surprising that both express a distaste for mystery. Forster sides more with Mrs. Moore; rationalist though he is in many ways, Forster has always been quick to acknowledge the presence of mystery both in the universe and in personal relationships, although muddle, when preventable, is for him one of the cardinal sins of mankind. A good deal of the horror of the novel arises precisely as muddle changes into its cosmic counterpart, chaos, and the lives of all the characters are undermined. At this point, however, all of this is not clear, and the conversation points rather to the mysteries and muddles that occur throughout the party.

These reach their climax when, Adela having regretted that she did not hear the Hindu Godbole sing, the Indian abruptly breaks out into a strange and disconcerting song. Having finished as casually as he had begun, Godbole tells his companions that they have just heard a religious song addressed by a milkmaiden to the god Krishna in which the god refuses to come. " 'But he comes in some other song, I hope?' said Mrs. Moore gently. 'Oh, no, he refuses to come,' repeated Godbole, perhaps not understanding her question. 'I say to Him, Come, come, come, come, come, come. He neglects to come' " (p. 84). Godbole's attitude, as expressed in his appearance, in his song, in his silences, is completely unnerving to the Westerners. The harmony of his presence is the outgrowth of his religious beliefs, of his entire approach to the universe. Feeling as he does, that everything ordinarily called reality is in fact illusion, he is able to recognize and to accept it all with an inclusiveness and a willingness impossible for the English. He is "Ancient Night"; he eludes the structures the Western minds have erected to accommodate reality to themselves. His affinities are with eternity, not time, with the one, not with the many, and in him the Westerners come upon something to which they are unaccoustomed and of which they are somehow afraid.

In fact, for Adela and, more immediately, for Mrs. Moore, Godbole's song marks a turning point in their own feelings and attitudes. Mrs. Moore's natural optimism, her feeling of oneness with her God and with the universe, and her desire to understand the foreign country to which she has come support her in the early part of her visit. Free of the rigid mentality of the Anglo-Indians, free even of the rational approach of Adela and Fielding, she is in some ways more able to assimilate new experience—to a point. The categories of her mind are more fundamental, more inclusive, but ultimately they, too, have their limits. She is still secure in her spiritual odyssey when she meets Aziz, but already doubts have begun to insinuate themselves. She begins to wonder, hesitantly, whether India is part of the earth she has always known, whether God is a force in India; she finds that the thought of God is with her more than it has ever been but also that it has never been less satisfying. Her mind centers more and more on her God because He is the foundation and center of her entire world view, but she is less and less comforted because she is falling victim to cultural relativism. She is unable to accept a way of life so totally different from her own, so strangely foreign in its most basic assumptions, and she comes, particularly after the party, to feel increasingly insecure about the entire universe.

Mrs. Moore's and Adela's "passage to India" and Aziz' friendships, no less than the order of the Anglo-Indian community, rest on weak foundations. To a smaller or larger degree they are all based on a false assumption of order in the universe, and they do not recognize, or cannot face, the disorder or chaos, even the variety, around them. All the meetings, all the attempts at communication are threatened by disruptive, disorderly, meaningless forces. Beneath all human efforts to give form to the world, to create civilization, lies, as the novel increasingly shows, nothing—no god, no first mover, no sustaining force.

The symbolism of "Mosque" is, as has been said, dual, and indeed, the more one studies the first section, the stronger the negative meaning of the symbol appears. Early in the book there are intimations of the difficulties that plague the man who seeks to mediate between Anglo-Indian rigidity and utter shapelessness. In one scene Forster describes the advanced young missionary who believes that in our Father's house there are mansions even for the monkeys and the jackals, but who becomes uneasy when his Indian friends ask whether there is not room as well for oranges, cactuses, crystals, and mud. With delicate and somewhat melancholy irony Forster presents the problem of inclusion and exclusion: any attempt to fix boundaries, to establish order, means that something or someone must be left out, and yet total inclusion is perhaps only another name for chaos. Forster does not say here what man can do, but the dilemma forms the background of all that henceforth happens in the book. Adrift in a formless sea, man is unable to get his bearings: in one direction he sees an infinite regression of human types; in another, jackals, wasps, and bacteria shading off into inanimate mud; in still another, endless sky—this last perhaps the most frightening of all, for there man seeks God and finds only *le silence des espaces infinis*. Throughout the novel there is a constant use of imagery meant to suggest the limitless beyond—arches beyond arches, vaults beyond vaults, echoes beyond echoes—stretching out past the stars to the blue sky, past the sky to some colorless and silent infinity.

Caught between the two infinities of the immeasurably small and the immeasurably large, the men and women of Chandrapore illustrate, in less dramatic and cosmic ways, the failure to communicate that follows inevitably from living in such a universe as Forster describes. Mrs. Moore is unable to explain to her son her feelings about God or men; Aziz fails to make contact with Godbole; the "bridge" party, meant to close for an afternoon the gap between the Indians and the English, ends as a dismal failure; even Fielding and Aziz encounter difficulties, difficulties which are overcome, significantly, not by words but once again by their intuitive and nonrational rapport.

The most interesting failure of communication, and one that bears on the problem of nonverbal relations, is that between Adela Quested and Ronny Heaslop. Adela is, one learns in *Howards End*, a member of the Schlegel circle, and one can surmise something of her character from this association with Margaret and Helen. Indeed it proves to be true that she is intelligent, intellectual, and eager in her pursuit of new experiences, but she is, in other ways, a far narrower person than either of the two sisters. "She goes on," Fielding says, "as if she's at a lecture—trying so hard to understand India and life, and occasionally taking a note" (p. 124). Nonetheless, despite her inadequate approach to the mystery and diversity of India and of the world, Adela is a likeable person; her motives and her relations with other people, insofar as she understands them, are straight forward and sincere. She is made to appear particularly admirable in contrast with Ronny, who is complacent about the British raj and not a little self-satisfied as well. In India, he does not see India, and he is at best only dimly conscious of the cultural differences he cannot help noticing. Ronny represents Anglo-India at its worst, or, Forster might say, at its most typical. Adela soon recognizes these qualities and, even sooner than she herself realizes, decides not to marry him.

The scene in which Adela tells Ronny of her decision is a curious one. Ronny, although upset, takes the news with outward composure, and Adela feels ashamed; in her dry fashion she tries to encourage him to talk the matter over, but he is too unhappy to continue the conversation. As they agree that they will remain friends, less explicable forces begin to operate in their relationship: they feel a wave of relief, then of tenderness, and finally they begin to feel lonely. That their frankness and coolness is, particularly on Ronny's part, largely a manner, a convention, does not occur to them; Ronny's anger and Adela's inquietude remain unacknowledged. The new tenderness that they experience derives not from personal affection but from a reaction of fear to their strange surroundings. Adela suddenly feels less desire to see India, and her life seems much emptier than it had been. When an influential Indian suggests that they come for a ride with him, Adela, anxious only not to cause Ronny more trouble, agrees to go. As they sit in the car, their loneliness increases; more and more Adela and Ronny feel small and insecure and find themselves drawn together:

The two young people conversed and felt unimportant. When the darkness began, it seemed to well out of the meagre vegetation, entirely covering the fields each side of them before it brimmed over the road. Ronny's face grew dim—an event that always increased her esteem of his character. Her hand touched his, owing to a jolt, and one of the thrills so frequent in the animal kingdom passed between them, and announced that all their difficulties were only a lover's quarrel. Each was too proud to increase the pressure, but neither withdrew it, and a spurious unity descended on them, as local and temporary as the gleam that inhabits a firefly. It would vanish in a moment, perhaps to reappear, but the darkness is alone durable. And the night that encircled them, absolute as it seemed, was itself only a spurious unity, being modified by the gleams of the day that leaked up round the edges of the earth, and by the stars. (p. 92)

The feeling that the passage conveys is of a universe that is, in some mysterious and sickly way, alive and hostile. Enclosed together and moving in a troubled darkness, Ronny and Adela do indeed join hands, not, however, through a real attraction for each other, but through a mutual reaction against the menacing night that surrounds them. And even that reaction is precipitated by an accident rather than by true sympathy and understanding: a chance jolt of the car brings them into contact and creates between them a unity as spurious as the night's.

Indeed another accident seals the bargain between them; change and chance are operative in the human world as well as in the vaster universe. The car suddenly hits a tree. The Indian and his Eurasian driver become excited and upset, but Ronny and Adela manage to remain calm. Their awareness of a common danger that they have faced and their admiration for each other's behavior confirms their new feelings, and they are, at Adela's request, engaged. One feels, of course, that the engagement can have no permanent effects, for the communication that is established has about it something factitious; its causes are local and temporary. Although the fact of man's aloneness remains, there is no permanent reason for Adela to seek security with Ronny or for him to seek it with her. Forster's disillusionment spreads over a larger area than usual: there is a breakdown in his last novel of communication of every kind, and the life of the body becomes as suspect as the life of the mind. If words prove altogether inadequate to create a bond between men, physical contact does so only in a deceptive fashion. Man, Forster seems to say with so many contemporary philosophers, is alone in a meaningless universe, and the awareness of the existential condition brings with it feelings of dread, of anguish, and of solitude. Ronny and Adela, vaguely as they are aware of all this, react precisely against these feelings.

In the last important scene of "Mosque," the failure of communication reaches its climax. Aziz, having fallen slightly ill, is visited by a number of his Mohammedan friends, by a Hindu doctor, and finally by Fielding. The scene describes the disgruntlements, the suspicions, and the pettiness of the men; arguments and bickering break out again and again. As the visitors prepare to leave, they feel a discontent that is more than matched by what they find outside the door. An intense heat has left the streets empty, and as the men walk out into them they lose not only their ability to communicate with each other, but the very qualities that make them human. Everything is antagonistic or indifferent; the burning heat threatens to melt away the boundaries of the little enclave man has established in the midst of chaos; squirrels and birds that seem to be expressing something but are understood neither by each other nor by men add their noises to the unquiet atmosphere. Insignificant man stands in the midst of millions of confused sounds and unknown creatures that care nothing for his plans and aspirations. Oddly, the men who leave Aziz' bungalow seem in some way closer together than are any of the other people in the novel, but the contact is only, and distressingly, physical. They are part of a common, molten mass, separated, to be sure, by pockets of dead, stagnant air, but commonly encircled by the vast inanimate world. Indeed the bond they share is so distressing that they hurry off on their separate ways, for they have lost their human attributes—and, if communication is difficult among men, it is still necessary first that there be men if there is to be communication.

With the cool weather passes whatever hope is expressed in the first section of the novel. "April, herald of horrors, is at hand" (p. 120). The sun that in the first pages of the book was the source of strength "was returning to his kingdom with

power but without beauty . . . he was merely a creature, like
the rest, and so debarred from glory" (p. 120). Everything—
sun, men, birds, squirrels—is reduced to the status of animal life
or simply to an amorphous mass; separateness is overcome only
at the cost of complete indistinction, indistinction only by the
loss of communication.

The section does not end quite so lugubriously or so heat-
edly, however, for Aziz calls Fileding back to speak to him and,
showing him a picture of his dead wife, thereby gives proof of
his friendship. Still, although his gesture robs the previous
scene of some of its terror, things are not as they were at their
first meeting. Fielding is flattered, but he feels old and dis-
consolate; he knows himself to be incapable of meeting Aziz
with equal emotion, incapable of exchanging equal confidences.
For his part, Aziz passes from an attitude of admiration to one
of patronage. He falls asleep, after Fielding leaves, thinking
that they are friends, brothers, but his thoughts fade, as always,
half into dreams; the image of Fielding is replaced by others,
finally by one of the ninety-nine attributes of God, inscribed,
black against white, under domes in eternal gardens. Part I
closes then with a return to a mosque, now not only, as at the
beginning, a symbol of meeting and friendship, but also, in the
light of all that has happened, perhaps even more of disruption,
disorder, and incommunicability. The cool weather has begun
to pass away and the structures that have hidden the abyss from
sight are ready to melt away.

II

Compared with the earlier novels, A *Passage to India* reveals a much more profound and elemental primitivism, a
primitivism that involves not only the usual comparison of two
cultures or of two ways of life, but of civilization as a whole
with whatever preceded it. The symbol of this earlier time is
not Italian *caffès* or English hills but what Forster calls "India
the primal," and that symbol is of emptiness and desolation
rather than of fuller and more natural life. If Forster looks about
him and dislikes what he sees in his twentieth-century world,

he looks back in his last novel to what was before the centuries as well and reacts with horror to what he sees there.

The second part of A *Passage to India*, "Caves," is given over to the expression of this more anarchic primitivism and to an indication of the effects on the characters of the vision it inspires. As in the other parts, so here the mood and themes are set in the first chapter, where, in his description of India, Forster attempts to universalize the setting in which his English and Indians move, thus giving symbolic meaning to the events that follow. Starting from the present, time, in the chapter, recedes further and further, becoming, as it does so, increasingly more cosmic: before man, before religion, before the Himalayas, ancient India is finally reabsorbed into the sun in the vast backward movement of Forster's prose. The history of man is not even alluded to, for it is as nothing when compared with India's; in the immense geologic evolution of which the great subcontinent is the sign, humanity is a speck on the ageless earth. In the beginning was India, and is; but India will not always be: the chapter moves forward now to an inconceivably remote future when all will again be lifeless and cold. As in the beginning, so at the end, there is no thought for man, too insignificant for consideration in the cosmic processes of the universe.

But the broad sweep of Forster's imaginings begins to narrow now, and the gigantic symbol of primal India shrinks to the corresponding symbol of the Marabar Caves, for man must stand in some relation to this universe of which he is so small and temporary a part, and that relation must be established with something he can more readily grasp. The Marabar Hills "are older than all spirit. . . . Even Buddha . . . shunned a renunciation more complete than his own, and has left no legend of struggle or victory in the Marabar" (p. 130). The hills lack all proportion, all order, relate to nothing else in the world. But the caves inside them are stranger still: all are alike, unornamented, indistinguishable one from the other. The visitor to the caves, Forster says, finds it difficult to say what kind of experience he has had, indeed whether he has had one at all.

Nothing, nothing attaches to them, and their reputation—for they have one—does not depend upon human speech. It is as if the surrounding plain or the passing birds have taken upon themselves to exclaim "extraordinary," and the word has taken root in the air, and been inhaled by mankind. (p. 130)

In fact, the caves are extraordinary precisely because they are so vacant, so tedious, so totally inexpressive; they seem ever to promise more than they fulfill, to suggest meanings that they do not yield. They recall Krishna, who does not come, or the Indian countryside in which there is not enough god to go around. Their effect is to frustrate the seeker, and yet their impact derives, not from anything so definite as evil, but from the repeated assertion of nothingness. "If mankind grew curious and excavated," Forster says of the numberless caves still unsealed, "nothing, nothing would be added to the sum of good or evil" (p. 131). If the hills are unspeakable, the caves are more so still, for in their hollowness, their monotony, and their evanescent beauty is revealed a truth about the universe that most men are unable to accept, but by which all men are affected. This truth becomes apparent in the expedition of a group of English and Indians to the Marabar and in the results of that visit.

The expedition is planned by Aziz and is intended as a splendid replica of Fielding's tea party. From the beginning the picnic is attended by innumerable petty troubles, but these are only the signs of a general malaise that afflicts the universe as a whole and Mrs. Moore and Adela in particular. Forster, speaking in his own person, expresses this malaise in its most general form when he says:

Most of life is so dull that there is nothing to be said about it . . . and though we continue to exclaim, "I do enjoy myself," or "I am horrified," we are insincere. "As far as I feel anything, it is enjoyment, horror"—it's no more than that really, and a perfectly adjusted organism would be silent. (p. 139)

Forster's words are frightening because, like the caves, they express, not a positive reaction to what is wrong with the world, but an awareness of emptiness, of nothingness. They strike out at the foundations of life rather than at its forms and thereby undermine all the structures built upon it.

The two women, of course, do not have so conscious an awareness of why they are troubled, but they are bothered nonetheless. Neither, Forster comments, had felt anything acutely since she heard Godbole's song; their feelings, however, are different. Both are vulnerable, but Mrs. Moore, no longer willing or able to fight against her intimations of life as meaningless, is more so; she begins to pass into apathy and cynicism. Adela is far more protected against herself than is her older friend, able as she is to devote herself to her passion for plans. As the train moves on to the picnic, Adela thinks of her accident, of Ronny, of her future life in the Anglo-Indian community, and yet even she cannot block out completely the noise of the wheels. Indistinctly she senses that the train is saying something to her but "its message—for it had one—avoided her well-equipped mind" (p. 142). As on the day when Fielding visited Aziz, the universe seems alive with sounds that cannot be understood or interpreted, and India itself, now that the hot season has arrived, adds to the confusion and the incommunicability everywhere. India "calls 'Come' through her hundred mouths, through objects ridiculous and august. But come to what? She has never defined. She is not a promise, only an appeal" (p. 143).

Everything disappoints the two women: the pointlessness of their surroundings, of what they are doing, of what all men are doing weighs upon them with increasing force. Nothing is real, nothing has meaning, there is only silence, failure, and unfulfillment. Mrs. Moore's apathy becomes the apathy of the world, and man's efforts an illusion, a castle of sand in the vast stretches of unrecorded time. At Aziz' suggestion they now enter a cave, and the visit proves horrible for Mrs. Moore. At first Forster suggests various physical reasons for her distress: the cave is too crowded and stuffy; Mrs. Moore, unable to breathe, becomes faint; an object strikes her face. But there is something else as well—an echo that terrifies her more than anything besides. "The echo in a Marabar cave . . ." Forster explains, "is entirely devoid of distinction. Whatever is said, the same monotonous noise replies, and quivers up and down the walls until it is absorbed into the roof. 'Boum' is the sound as far as the human alphabet can express it, or 'bou-oum,' or 'ou-boum,'—utterly dull. Hope, politeness, the blowing of a nose, the squeak of a boot, all produce 'boum'" (p. 154).

More and more, as she thinks over her experience, the echo comes to be the most important and frightening thing in it. It is in a way an intensification of the feeling she had had when approaching the Marabar: everything appears to be cut off at its root; life goes on but has no consequences. Yet worse is to come. The echo begins to resound with still more general significance: "Suddenly, at the edge of her mind, Religion appeared, poor little talkative Christianity, and she knew that all its divine words from 'Let there be Light' to 'It is finished' only amounted to 'boum' . . . and she realized that she didn't want . . . to communicate with anyone, not even with God" (p. 157). In the face of so many and so diverse customs, cultures, and religions, the old woman is unable to retain her belief in an ordered world overseen by the Christian God; confronted by Mohammedanism, by Hinduism, by an India so different from the tidier England she has known, she succumbs, fully now, to the blight of relativism.[5] Her cosmos is shattered and she withdraws into all that is left her as solid and substantial— into herself. Her desire to communicate disappears, and she sinks into a profound state of cynical indifference, able only barely to keep herself from complete engulfment.[6]

Mrs. Moore's experience is the climax of the novel. In it are realized all the intimations of disquietude in the world and in the relations between men that were suggested in "Mosque"

5 On this subject, see Professor Austin Warren's excellent article, "E. M. Forster," *Rage for Order* (Chicago: University of Chicago Press, 1948), p. 129.

6 Forster seems to be indicating quite clearly that Mrs. Moore's experience is not personal only, that it is not restricted even to Western and Christian minds alone. In trying to establish a bond between the elderly Englishwoman and the Indians (cf. Aziz' remark: "Then you are an Oriental," and the fact that, in Part I, Mrs. Moore is aware of a secret known only to the non-English, "a racial secret communicable more by blood than speech" [p. 103]), Forster is pointing to a more universal significance in her collapse of values. To be sure, the English are most vulnerable in India, but there seems every reason to believe that what lies beneath their structures lies beneath those of the Indians as well. Mrs. Moore's experience takes place at a picnic given by a Mohammedan and in a cave that is associated with a heterodox Hindu sect. The abyss lies at the feet of all men, and it is into that abyss that Mrs. Moore peers. Her vision is of chaos, of chaos in the social and religious spheres first, but more fundamentally, of chaos underlying all of man's various efforts at civilization.

and in the first part of "Caves." The meaning of the experience is somewhat modified and enlarged later in the book, but its essential truth is established: Mrs. Moore's echo begins to spread and has its effects not only on herself but on those around her as well. The first one to be in some way affected by Mrs. Moore's visit to the cave is Adela Quested. As a result of the older woman's indisposition, she goes off to visit another cave with only Aziz and a native guide. Thinking about her impending marriage and realizing suddenly that she doesn't love Ronny, she enters a cave alone and imagines that someone is attempting to rape her. She scrambles down the mountainside and, in a state of shock and exhaustion, returns to town with an Anglo-Indian woman whom she meets. Aziz is unaware of what has happened, and so the party goes on, all apparently in order; nothing is suspected until the train arrives back in Chandrapore and Aziz is immediately arrested.

It is discovered that Adela, too, has been frightened by an echo, and it is that fact which most clearly links her experience with Mrs. Moore's. Superficially the two are quite different, Adela's being more readily explainable in psychological terms. Forster lays fully the bases for the belief that Adela has suffered a hallucination, induced by her confused and repressed thoughts about love and marriage. He indicates even the possibility of sun-stroke. But the echo remains, and one is led to feel that, whatever the external causes of Adela's delusion, the more fundamental ones lie, for her as for Mrs. Moore, in the breakdown of her ability to cope with the strangeness around her. The rigidity of her view of life keeps it partly intact, but fundamentally it, too, is undermined by an echo from the abyss, and it is by way of Adela that the echo now begins to work its evil throughout the entire community.

Adela's accusation and Aziz' arrest are the public counterparts of the more private experiences that Mrs. Moore and Adela herself have in the caves; they are secondary and derived echoes of the original "boum," which has never ceased to reverberate. Fielding, as soon as he begins to speak to the English officials, knows that something other than the ostensible situation is wrong. "He felt that a mass of madness had arisen and tried to overwhelm them all; it had to be shoved back into its

pit somehow, and he didn't know how to do it, because he did
not understand madness" (p. 170). And Fielding does not understand either what the connection is between "the evil [that]
was propagating in every direction" (p. 195) and the ultimate
nothingness of the caves, the indistinction in which good and
evil are the same. It is Godbole who solves this problem, Godbole who (perhaps announcing the truth promised by the
Siren) appears at rare but important intervals in the book to
shed light on what Forster is trying to say. He tells Fielding:

Good and evil are different, as their names imply. But, in my own
humble opinion, they are both of them aspects of my Lord. He is
present in the one, absent in the other, and the difference between
presence and absence is great, as great as my feeble mind can
grasp. Yet absence implies presence, absence is not non-existence,
and we are therefore entitled to repeat, "Come, come, come, come."
(p. 186)

Godbole's Hinduism does not represent Forster's own point
of view, but it is a clue to it, as here, where the connection between absence and evil is made explicit. So for Forster, the
chaos of the abyss has by that very quality the power of evil in
relation to man's attempts to order his world. It is important
to determine just what Forster is about. The attacks on false
order in "Mosque" are clearly not intended as an exaltation of
disorder; the vision of chaos in "Caves" is altogether fearful, but
—and this seems to be one of Forster's main points—one gains
nothing by shirking knowledge of what is true; indeed one loses
a good deal. Something more positive comes later in the novel,
after the evil has been forced back into its box, and is suggested
in Godbole's speech, which ends, however feebly, on what is a
note of hope. Godbole, almost alone in the novel, is able both
to accept a pessimistic view of the universe and to continue to
live in some sort of purposeful way. For the moment, however,
evil is still very much loose in the universe.

As soon as Adela returns, the Anglo-Indian community
takes its stand: if Fielding's object is to shove madness back into
its pit, the object of most of the English is to embrace it with
open arms. Confirmed in their bad opinions of the Indians,
they huddle still more tightly together in their English settle-
ment and prepare to repulse the barbarian hordes, whose coming

they await with confidence and, perhaps, not without satisfaction.

For Fielding, too, the cave has its echoes, murmurs of failure, incompleteness, limitation, and even as he begins his struggle against the evil emanating from the Marabar, he falls, in part, a victim to it. Mrs. Moore, of course, remains too affected by her original experience, too shocked by the terror of her vision, to assist in the fight against its results, while Adela feels somehow that only the older woman can help her. Slightly fevered, her skin full of cactus spines, abnormally sensitive to any bodily contact, Adela submits patiently to the oversolicitous ministrations of the Anglo-Indian women, longing to speak to Mrs. Moore, who refuses to visit her. A little phrase recurs to her again and again: " 'In space things touch, in time things part,' she repeated to herself while the thorns were being extracted—her brain so weak that she could not decide whether the phrase was a philosophy or a pun" (p. 201). The words are in fact a comment on Adela's own experiences in India, on her engagement to Ronny, induced as it was by the spurious unity they felt in the face of the empty universe and their own physical contact; and on her sudden awareness that she did not love him, that the emotion they felt was destined to pass, to give way before the separateness that follows from the impermanency and flux of all things in time. For a moment, in space, men can share a common awareness of the human condition, but in time incommunicability reasserts itself and divides them from each other as they are separated also from animals and from the inanimate universe.

Adela's desire to see Mrs. Moore seems to involve an awareness that the older woman possesses some powers she herself lacks, powers capable, as reason does not appear to be, of dealing with the aftermath of the echo, and so she looks forward anxiously to meeting her friend again. But she is disappointed in her expectations: the old woman greets her perfunctorily, withdraws her hand from Adela's grasp, and begins immediately to speak about going home. Adela feels obscurely that Mrs. Moore is repelled by her, particularly when she is asking her questions. And she is right. Mrs. Moore's bitterness and disillusionment, which extend to God, to love, and to personal relationships, seem particularly strong in relation to the possibility of communication. She is most annoyed, most contemptuous, when she is asked to explain herself in words, and yet she manages somehow to convey to Adela her feeling that Aziz is innocent, that he is good. That she does so indicates a curious contradiction in Mrs. Moore's attitudes and points to the seriousness of the crisis she is undergoing. Her outward actions are marked by complete disregard for others' feelings and by a self-centered interest only in her own welfare; the truth of her vision is vitiated by an excessive acerbity that makes her incapable of any generosity or sympathy. And yet, on some deeper level, her more fundamental interest in people and her desire to love them and see them happy assert themselves and make themselves known in mysterious ways. Her regard for Aziz penetrates through her indifference and her blasphemy, since, in confirming Adela's own doubts about the incident, she is preparing for his ultimate vindication. The knowledge must be communicated without words, from some depth unaffected by the shattering of her world picture, but it is communicated.

Still, Mrs. Moore cannot, placed as she is, do any more, either for others or for herself. Ronny suggests that she leave before the trial, and she agrees without enthusiasm. At Chandrapore, Mrs. Moore remains in the grip of her vision of emptiness and negation, and she prepares to leave India, disillusioned, unkind, pursued still by the relentless echo from the Marabar. Something, however, happens to her as she travels across India to her boat. She is alone, and she finds her freedom from memories of the past pleasant. The weather is temporarily a little cooler, and the journey proves agreeable. For the first time since her arrival, there is beauty around her. More important still, she begins to regain a sense of objectivity; the world changes from a phantasmagoric reflection of her own sense of flux into a more stable world of objects. Life seems to her indestructible, though changing, and asserts its independence of her particular view of it. Her bitterness begins to decrease. The trip continues, and, by the time she reaches Bombay, Mrs. Moore feels that she has not been in the right places. She thinks of the marvels of India that she has not seen, and she feels the desire to overcome her destructive experience of relativism. Suddenly she realizes that she does not have the final answer after all, that she has allowed her vision to simplify the universe. She learns that what she saw in the caves was true, but that it was not all.

The passages describing Mrs. Moore's trip are often overlooked,[7] but, in fact, they constitute the turning point of the novel: in them is intimated Forster's counterstatement to the message of the Marabar, which is developed through the rest of the novel, particularly in the third part. But it is equally wrong to overestimate what they are saying, to assume that the vision of the caves is canceled. Mrs. Moore was, in fact, not wrong in what she saw, but wrong in the way she saw it, wrong not in assuming that beneath all man's efforts there lies an abyss, but in refusing to go on despite (but not ignoring) the fact. *La vie humaine commence de l'autre côté du désespoir.* Man must indeed go beyond, must build his structures, must work for civilization, but he must do so with an awareness of the absence of any absolute foundations or guarantees. The position is a difficult one, the balance hard to achieve, and it is not until the end of the novel that one can judge accurately where exactly Forster himself stands. Nonetheless, it is clear that Mrs. Moore has managed to come some distance out of the abyss, and, as the echo which she first heard began immediatety to affect those around her, so now, even without her presence, her new knowledge, which allows once more for belief in love and kindness, starts to dissipate the evil that is loose in Chandrapore and helps the effort that eventually pushes madness back into its pit.

But Mrs. Moore's influence, though it succeeds in changing the course of events, is not able to stop those events altogether. Even before leaving Chandrapore, she had said of Adela: "She has started the machinery; it will work to its end" (p. 215), and now, after her departure, matters approach their climax. The heat and the dust increase, and with them the bad tempers of both the Indians and the English who are involved in the trial. From the moment of Adela's entrance into the courtroom odd things begin to happen, at times to her, at times to the

7 But see Beer, pp. 158–59 and Crews, p. 159.

crowd at large; in inscrutable and irrational ways good begins to assert its power against evil and to repel it. The first of the incidents has no obvious relation to what is going on in the room: Adela's eye is attracted by the punkah wallah, the man who pulls the fan above the heads of the spectators. Connected with the lowest stratum of human life, the splendid punkah wallah rises in Adela's imagination to godlike stature. Above and below human concerns, symbol of an impersonal fate and of something more fundamental than reason, "a winnower of souls" (p. 226), as Forster calls him, he has a peculiar effect on Adela. The untouchable Indian is somehow akin to the enigma of the universe, and Adela is led to question her opinions and her reason for being there. Her mind begins to broaden, to take account of the claims of other cultures, but her relativistic position has another effect on her mind than it did on Mrs. Moore's. Her dry rationalism begins to give way, and, thinking of Mrs. Moore, she begins to see more truly, in terms of her own experience, the world around her.

The trial begins. An argument soon develops over Mrs. Moore, the defense claiming that she has not been allowed to give her evidence. One of Aziz' lawyers dramatically leaves the courtroom, and spontaneously Mrs. Moore's name is picked up by the onlookers and then by the people outside, becoming transformed and Indianized into Esmiss Esmoor. Ronny puts forth reasons to explain the incident: his mother had spoken about the Marabar in her sleep, and her words had been picked up by native servants and sold to the defense. But something more mysterious seems to lie at the source of the incident, and it is later learned that Mrs. Moore had died at sea before the trial. Like Mrs. Wilcox, Mrs. Moore continues to affect the living after her own death: her spirit is abroad, the spirit of the Mrs. Moore who had come to recognize the incompleteness of the vision in the cave. Her influence remains in the courtroom, where the final result of her experience in the Marabar is being enacted, and through Adela brings it to an unexpected conclusion.

As her lawyer begins to question her, Adela is curiously affected: "She didn't think what had happened, or even remember in the ordinary way of memory, but she returned to the Marabar Hills, and spoke from them across a sort of darkness" (p. 236). The examination continues, Adela answering with her new insight into what happened that day, until the lawyer asks whether Aziz followed her into the cave. Half her mind back at the actual scene, she waits to see Aziz enter the cave, but he does not come. She asks for time to think, but still she remains alone and finally announces that Aziz did not follow her. Tension mounts in the courtroom and "something that she did not understand took hold of the girl and pulled her through. Though the vision was over, and she had returned to the insipidity of the world, she remembered what she had learnt. Atonement and confession—they could wait. It was in hard prosaic tones that she said, 'I withdraw everything'" (p. 239).

The trial is over, Aziz is cleared, and to that extent the echo from the Marabar Cave is silenced. As the discomfited English and the exultant Indians leave the room, madness seems to have been overcome, but how much has actually been accomplished? It is clear that good has triumphed, but once again through the agency of recondite and inarticulate forces—the punkah wallah, the travestied syllables of Mrs. Moore's name, and Adela's vision. That Mrs. Moore's spirit is the chief factor in clearing up the muddle seems a reassertion of the values for which she stood before her experience in the cave—love, friendship, and intuitive understanding—but it remains to be seen how effective her spiritual influence proves, and nothing occurs to reassert the values of reason or verbal communication. "Speech was more difficult than vision" (p. 238), Forster comments at the point when Adela tries to express her new understanding of the incident in the cave, and it remains more difficult even after the trial. The complete nullity of the Marabar has been dissipated, but life is not by any means what it once seemed to be when Mrs. Moore and Adela first came to India; even the first exultation that follows Adela's announcement is moderated in the more prosaic events that follow, while the united crowd of Indians who stream from the court eventually become once again separate and separated men. The echo is not really dead, nor will it ever die completely: affirmation is never so strong as to overcome negation in A *Passage to India*, and though there are many ways of reacting to the abyss, some good, some bad, nothing can gainsay completely its existence or its power.

The trial once over, the various characters are left with the job of re-establishing their lives, in so far as they can, on their old bases, or better, of reconstructing them along improved lines. Not unexpectedly the larger Anglo-Indian situation remains much the same; there is still the necessity for kindness and more kindness, and the Anglo-Indians are incapable of giving it. On a more personal level, the friendship of Fielding and Aziz begins to be infected by misunderstanding and distrust. The atmosphere of celebration provides a less effective binding force than did the feeling of crisis, and the two men come to be aware of differences between them and to be troubled by them. They break finally over the question of Adela: Fielding is shocked to find that his friend intends to ask for heavy damages from the girl, while Aziz, although he is finally convinced by Fielding, comes to suspect that the Englishman, motivated throughout by self-interest, intends to marry Adela for her money. So the friendship between the two men ends, partly because of real differences of opinion, but much more because of differences of temperament and mutual misinterpretations. Mrs. Moore had been able to bring East and West into the compass of her instinctive sympathy, but Fielding, for all his goodwill, is incapable of reaching Aziz.

There is some consolation in the new relationship between Fielding and Adela, a relationship quite different from the one Aziz imagines. One recognizes in Adela a new and more admirable honesty toward herself and others, and, despite himself, Fielding finds that he likes her better. Both are somewhat wiser people than they once were. Dependent still upon their reason, they are willing to admit its limitations: the riddle of the cave is left unsolved, not forced into a rational interpretation, and both are willing to admit that there is mystery in the universe. They are more stable and better individuals, not necessarily happier ones. As Forster describes their new rapport, he comments: "A friendliness, as of dwarfs shaking hands, was in the air" (p. 274). Fielding and Adela are smaller people too, and although they agree they want to go on living, they do so with a sense of incompleteness and dissatisfaction that seems the inevitable counterpart of their admirable but limited rationalism and of their integrity.

As Mrs. Moore's return trip modifies the pessimism of her experience in the Marabar and counteracts some of its results, so the events that follow the trial warn against an excess of optimism. If cynicism and apathy, if bleak and hollow despair, are not the proper reactions to the universe, still that universe nourishes misunderstandings and imposes limitations. The one certain answer that emerges from "Caves" is that man must, as best he can, go on despite his knowledge of the abyss, must, indeed, go on with knowledge of it, but this answer is singularly bare. It requires to be supplemented by more positive indications of how man is to make the best of his lonely and imperfect world, and before the second part of the novel is over Forster does hint at other possibilities.

The first of these emerges in a conversation between Fielding and Aziz. "There is something in religion," Fielding says, "that may not be true, but has yet to be sung. . . . Something that the Hindus have perhaps found." And then he adds, "Hindus are unable to sing" (p. 288). Fielding's remarks are, in a sense, another recognition on his part of the limits of his rational approach, of the depths in the universe he is unable to fathom. His mention of Hinduism looks back to Godbole's song and to his discourse on good and evil, and, even more, looks forward to the third part of the book, which is devoted, for the most part, to the examination of whatever it is that Hindus have found. It is in this way that Mrs. Moore's spirit continues to play a part in the novel, for it is she, more than any of the other characters in the book, who is in sympathy with the spirit of Indian religion, and it is through her and Godbole that Forster conveys his message of love and instinctive understanding.

But Forster indicates also a way other than Mrs. Moore's, which relies most on inclusion, and that is Fielding's, the way of form and order. As in Mrs. Moore's case, so in Fielding's, the revelation of a fuller approach to life comes as the result of a journey, and, if her revelation is more fully worked out (as it is in Part III), his ideal gathers strength from being the only one in the book that is at no time criticized. When he comes to Venice, he feels about its buildings that:

[They] stood in the right place, whereas in poor India everything was placed wrong. He had forgotten the beauty of form among idol temples and lumpy hills; indeed, without form, how can there be beauty? . . In the old undergraduate days he had wrapped himself up in the many-coloured blanket of St. Mark's, but something more precious than mosaics and marbles was offered to him now: the harmony between the works of man and the earth that upholds them, the civilization that has escaped muddle, the spirit in a reasonable form, with flesh and blood subsisting. (p. 293)

It is in this passage, if anywhere in the book, that Forster returns to the spirit of the earlier novels, particularly of *Howards End*. Here again is the love for the "natural order" of Italy, the love for moderation, for proportion; it is Margaret Schlegel's ideal of connection, made manifest in the outward symbols of an entire civilization. Here Forster comes closest to Fielding, and both, while condemning the "false order" of Anglo-India or of Christianity, shrink, too, from the formlessness of India. It is difficult in *A Passage to India* to say where, ultimately, Forster's sympathies lie, but it cannot be doubted that there is an enthusiasm and a straightforward affirmation in this description that is not found in the rest of the book. It is important, therefore, while reading the third, the "Hindu" section of the novel, to remember Fielding's reaction to Venice, and not to simplify Forster's view of life into merely an affirmation of subrational communication: form, harmony, and reason receive, this once at least, their tribute as well.

If the ideal put forth here is not the ideal of the book as a whole, it is not that Forster longs any less for the "Mediterranean harmony," but that, like Mrs. Moore, he is himself troubled by an awareness of the welter and multiplicity of the world's cultures and beliefs. And though Forster may himself prefer the answer Italy offers, he cannot ignore the people outside the Mediterranean world. Venice is an ideal only for the West, perhaps only for those whose lands border on "that exquisite lake," and therefore *A Passage to India* does not end as did *A Room with a View*, to the music of the melting snows passing into the Mediterranean, but to the sounds of less harmonious and civilized music, in India, the land of man in his most basic, if not his most accomplished, state.

III

Part III of the novel, "temple," does indeed open in India, not now in Chandrapore, but in Mau, a Hindu native state, and opens in the midst of a festival celebrating the birth of the god Krishna. The chapter that describes this festival serves not only to introduce the themes and symbols that are to be developed, as do the first chapters of the earlier sections, but is itself the most important and colorful scene in Part III. A *Passage to India* may be said to consist of a series of tableaux, held together by the overlapping of the three main symbols of the book—the mosque, the caves, the temple—and by various "rhythms"; of these tableaux the one devoted to the birth of Krishna is, deservedly, among the most famous. In it Forster combines skillfully an appreciation of the Hindu spirit with an ironic, Western detachment, so that the reader is made to move now closer to, now further from, the center of the event, alternately sympathizing with and criticizing, but always understanding, the strange ceremony.

To a large degree the things Forster finds to praise in the Hindu spirit are precisely those he finds absent in the West. "Religion," he comments, "is a living force to the Hindus, and can at certain moments fling down everything that is petty and temporary in their natures" (p. 316). In the Hindu ceremony, religion is a response of the total personality to something larger than itself, to the mystery of the universe, a response that recalls most clearly Mr. Emerson's in *A Room with a View*. And, again like Mr. Emerson, the Hindus who participate in the ceremony feel no need for gravity: their merriment is opposed to the asceticism and the solemnity of Christianity, and indeed it is the inclusiveness of Hinduism that Forster most admires, its ability to hold together all the seemingly irreconcilable feelings and desires of men. In its spirit men are able, if only for a while, to love each other and the universe they symbolize in their god.

Forster does note, however, that the ceremony is a triumph

of intuition, and to that extent there is no room for reason in what is otherwise a unified and complete response. In fact, increasingly, even as he reaches the climax of the ceremony, the moment when all men come together, Forster begins to point to the less admirable or acceptable side of Hinduism: the exaltation that overwhelms the believers is temporary and its effects pass with the ceremony. Even the inclusiveness that is symbolized by the Krishna festival has its troubling side: it is in some ways dangerously near to chaos, to the horror Mrs. Moore saw in the Marabar.[8] The problem of inclusion and exclusion arises again. Forster's Hindus, like his Italians, shun asceticism and rigidity, but they do not have the "natural order" of the Mediterranean people. The Hindu order is so large as to be almost shapeless. "They did not one thing which the non-Hindu would feel dramatically correct," Forster observes; "this approaching triumph of India was a muddle (as we call it), a frustration of reason and form" (pp. 296–97). And later, commenting on one of the signs before the altar, written in English to symbolize the universality of the god, and bearing the confused motto, "God si love," Forster asks, "Is this the final message of India?" (p. 297).

And indeed what is the final message for Forster, as he dramatizes it in the final section of his novel? The question is an important one, since it has often been assumed that the final answer to the vision of the caves lies in a total affirmation of Hinduism.[9] Forster did not, I think, intend such an affirmation, and certainly he has not produced one. To be sure, he admires the inclusiveness, the vitality, and the antiascetic attitude of the Hindus, but he is acutely aware of the muddle, the confusion, and the transitory nature of the ceremony that symbolizes their response to life. To the extent that his attitude can be said to be the Hindu one, it involves the recognition that man must have some relation with the unexplained and unexplainable,

8 Forster told the present writer that the Hindu festival represents the same thing as the scene in the cave, "turned inside out."

9 For other arguments against the idea that Forster is presenting Hinduism as a complete answer, see Crews, pp. 151–55, and the excellent article by David Shusterman, "The Curious Case of Professor Godbole: *A Passage to India* Re-examined," *PMLA*, LXXVI (September, 1961), 426–35.

albeit a relation never totally satisfactory. Godbole has from the beginning an attitude that comes only gradually to Mrs. Moore: the awareness that inadequacy and incompleteness are indelible features of the universe, but that one must go on nonetheless. In that both Godbole and Forster are, to a large extent, pessimistic about this world but convinced that man must do his best with what he is given, the comparison is legitimate.

Still, Forster is by no stretch of the imagination a Hindu, and if his remarks in A Passage to India are not sufficient proof of his disagreement, one may turn for confirmation to The Hill of Devi, a collection of letters that Forster sent home from India in 1912–13 and in 1921. One section of the correspondence of 1921, "Gokul Ashtami," is devoted to a description of the Krishna festival. In basic detail the account is very similar to the one in the novel, but the tone and observation of the former are a good deal more critical. One remark will indicate Forster's general feeling: "I do like Islam, though I have had to come through Hinduism to discover it. After all the mess and profusion and confusion of Gokul Ashtami, where nothing ever stopped or need ever have begun, it was like standing on a mountain" (p. 193). The generally sympathetic treatment of the ceremony in the novel points much more to Forster's skill as an artist than to his enthusiasm for what occurs. He is interested in what the religion represents to a Western mind, and he is criticizing Christianity at least as much as he is affirming Hinduism. Forster's interest in fact is in correcting the West, not in converting it to the East.

The "Temple," then, through its connection with the Hindu festival, becomes like the other symbols in the book, a dual or, better, an ambivalent symbol. It is in one aspect a reaffirmation of Mrs. Moore's vision while crossing the Indian continent, and in another a grotesque monument of the muddle that is described in the book. It signifies not that all is right in the world—quite the contrary—but that there are possibilities of constructive action. It signifies, too, that these possibilities are always subject to frustration, but, at any rate, the affirmation implicit in the symbol is stronger than that in the symbol of "Caves," where negation is uppermost. The rest of the section is devoted to a working out of the two meanings of "Temple," a balancing of hope and despair, as in all Forster's novels, an attempt that fails here only in that it is not sufficiently developed. Of the Hindu festival Forster has said: "It was architecturally necessary. I needed a lump, or a Hindu temple if you like—a mountain standing up. It is well placed; and it gathers up some strings. But there ought to be more after it. The lump sticks out a little too much." [10] The self-criticism is just; the festival scene does pick up strings left loose in Part II, but it absorbs too much of the space and interest of the third section. Therein seems to lie the explanation of the fact that critics have at times overemphasized the importance of the Hindu element in the book: the fault is in large part Forster's and it is a structural one. One must look to the other side of the "mountain standing up" to discover where exactly Forster intended to lead his readers.

It is the negative meaning of "Temple" that is first apparent after the festival. Forster makes it clear that discord still exists, not only between Indians and English, not only between Mohammedans and Hindus, but within Hinduism itself: "The fissures in the Indian soil are infinite" (p. 304). On a personal level, there is no real meeting in the confrontation of Aziz, now a doctor in Mau, and Fielding, who is making an educational survey for the government and traveling with his wife and brother-in-law (Mrs. Moore's children Ralph and Stella). Fielding is older, sterner, more official, Aziz hostile and guarded, and their conversation goes badly. The encounter ends with a complete separation between the two men, but Aziz "returned to the house excited and happy" (p. 315). Happy is a word that at this point applies to a state of which Aziz is not yet aware: as far as he is conscious of his attitude, he feels himself still angry and hurt, but within him the almost magic name of Mrs. Moore, which has entered the conversation, is beginning to produce its effect, just at the time when the Hindus prepare for the procession that is the aftermath of the festival celebrating the birth of Krishna.

The conjunction is significant: the spirit of Mrs. Moore and the spirit of Hinduism begin to work together toward the

10 Furbank and Haskell, p. 28.

same goal—reconciliation and unity. Once again the weather is propitious; it is the rainy season, the most favorable time of the Indian year. Everywhere the cycle of death and life is about to culminate in rebirth, the rebirth of nature, of the god (for to many of the Hindus the procession, rather than the earlier ceremony, symbolizes the birth of Krishna), and of personal relations. In Mau the atmosphere is charged with anticipation, and the time is ready, not indeed for the eradication of all the evil in the world and all difficulties among men, but for some adjustment between man's recognition of chaos and his ideals.

It is Aziz who proves to be the instrument of reconciliation. Alone, as he thinks, in the guest house where Fielding and his party are staying, he suddenly hears a voice that is familiar to him; [11] it is Ralph Moore's, and on to him Aziz projects all his anger at the English. But in the midst of their conversation Aziz unwittingly remarks to the boy that he is an Oriental and suddenly realizes that these are the words he had once said to his mother. The cycle has begun again. Ralph, like his sister, is attracted to Hinduism and, like her, he is distinctly his mother's child. Aziz is aware of the resemblance and begins to feel for the boy all he had felt for the old woman. As this instinctive communication is set up, intangible forces begin to operate. He offers to take Ralph out for a while onto the tank where the festivities are taking place. As they row, they hear the chanting of the Hindus and, among the syllables, the words "esmiss esmoor." They approach the celebrants and find themselves in the midst of a divine muddle: a model of the village of Gokul, Krishna's birthplace, is made ready to float upon the waters of the tank. It is set adrift by a naked Indian, the counterpart of the punkah wallah of the trial scene. Like the Indian of Chandrapore, he is an inscrutable fate: as he pushes the village out into the waters, his influence combines with those of Mrs. Moore and of the Hindu ceremony, and Aziz' boat collides with Fielding's, which is also out on the tank. "That was the climax,"

11 It is, of course, Ralph's voice that Aziz hears, but it reminds him of Mrs. Moore's. In *The Longest Journey* Rickie hears his mother's voice in his brother's, and Forster comments that a voice may be transmitted from generation to generation. In his interview with Angus Wilson, Forster made a point of saying (p. 54) that Mrs. Moore's influence does reappear in Part III of the novel.

Forster remarks, "as far as India admits of one" (p. 329). The climax is formless, shapeless, but it has its effect upon the English and upon Aziz. Once again Aziz and Fielding are friends, and for the first time Fielding and his wife are completely compatible. It is significant that ultimately an accident is required to bring about the reconciliations, an accident that is the last link in the chain of forces made up of the mysterious influences of Mrs. Moore, Krishna, and the naked Indian. Strange, inexplicable powers have succeeded where Fielding's reasonable attitudes failed. But the accident is different from the one that brought Ronny and Adela together. Here there is not a spurious unity but, Forster would have us believe, a spirit of genuine love: the forcible meeting of the occupants of the boats engenders a triumph of understanding and affection, and indeed the whole festival builds up to a reassertion of the possibility of personal relations. Aziz, Fielding, Ralph, and Stella themselves undergo a baptism by water. Like the Hindus, they are purged of suspicion, hatred, and pettiness; the reconciliations are genuine. But the question remains: Can they last, or will Aziz and the English, like the Hindus, revert to more normal patterns of behavior? Are the fissures in the Indian soil too deep to be mended by the forces of love and harmony?

The somewhat ambiguous answer to that question is given in the final scene of the book, in which, as in the comparable section of *Howards End*, there is much giving with one hand and taking back with the other. The festival is over and the focus of the last chapter is on Fielding and Aziz, on personal relations, and on the more limited, but more human, capacities of Islam and the West. To be sure, the re-establishment of good relations between the two men is due, in the first instance, to the influence of Hinduism (and Mrs. Moore), but it is clear that, if these relations are to continue, Aziz and Fielding must rely upon themselves. There is sadness in the last pages of the book, but it is sadness rather than the apathy and despair of "Caves." The two men are friends once more—the lines of communication have been repaired—but they know, too, that they cannot see each other again, that the ride they are taking through the Mau jungles will be their last. So brief a reconciliation is, perhaps, basis for small comfort, but in the light of what has gone before it is a triumph of sorts. It is an affirmation, however weak, of the possibility of personal relations, an answer, however limited, to the echo of the Marabar.

Of course, one must not make too much of this answer; the forces of disunion are still powerful, and they become more prominent as the men continue their ride. Both Fielding and Aziz are, and they realize the fact, different from what they were in Chandrapore. Talking about what means most to them, the two men find the conversation floundering; friendship is there, but communication is still difficult. Aziz tells Fielding to talk about something else, and for the rest of the ride they argue politics. The scene is strange; both become angry and excited. They speak more as an Englishman and an Indian than as Fielding and Aziz, and yet they are never closer. Excitement—in large part artificially generated—brings what sincerity and self-revelation cannot, a vital, if temporary, bond between them. They ride on, and "the divisions of daily life were returning" (p. 335), Forster comments in passing. But the curious conversation is prolonged a while longer by yet more intense insults and exacerbated emotions: Aziz begins to shout, and, when Fielding mocks him, he is beside himself with rage. Now, as both transcend their normal selves, as they pass beyond reason into a realm where, perhaps, communication is possible, the climax of their meeting comes. Aziz cries: " 'If it's fifty-five hundred years we shall get rid of you . . . and then'—he rode against him furiously—'and then,' he concluded, half kissing him, 'you and I shall be friends' " (pp. 335–36). But the moment cannot last; consummated in movement (like Adela's and Ronny's), fanned by the wing of a passing emotion, denying the facts that make for separation, it is, of its own nature and by necessity, transitory. Why can't they be friends now, Fielding asks;

But the horses didn't want it—they swerved apart; the earth didn't want it, sending up rocks through which riders must pass single file; the temples, the tank, the jail, the palace, the birds, the carrion, the Guest House, that came into view as they issued from the gap and saw Mau beneath: they didn't want it, they said in their hundred voices. "No, not yet," and the sky said, "No, not there." (p. 336)

Professor Brower has said of these final words that "the implication of a celestial 'Sometime, Somewhere' is inescapable. . . . The vision of the Caves is too compelling to be forgotten or to allow us to find solace in pleasing 'hints of infinity.'" [12] But though the words do imply the possibility of hope deferred to some distant future—that is the pattern of all Forster's novels —it is not necessary that the possibility be considered "celestial" or unreal, not, at any rate, if the hope is accepted, as I believe it is meant to be, as moderate and limited. The vision of the caves *is* compelling, and Forster does not mean for us to forget it. The abyss remains, no matter what man does, but man can do something nonetheless; he can attempt neither to deny it nor to give in to its horror, as Mrs. Moore did at first. He must, as Mrs. Moore later realized, give what meaning he can to his chaotic, orderless world, through his own, unaided efforts. The last chapter of the novel shows, indeed, that such an effort will never be easy; the forces of disorder are powerful and persistent, but they can be fought against and partially subdued, if not conquered. Forster's hope is hard won: it is founded upon despair, and its reliance is, ultimately, upon man himself.

A Passage to India is a novel of many impressive qualities, but probably the most impressive of them all lies in the complexity of the vision that it finally communicates. One can point —perhaps too readily—to the bleak despair of Mrs. Moore's experience in the Marabar Cave and to the wild harmony of the Hindu festival—indeed these are central moments. But the total effect of the novel is probably more dependent upon those scenes, and they constitute the majority, in which it is less easy to find a dominant mood. In them the sounds that anticipate and follow from the "boum" of the cave mingle with those generated by the "secret understanding of the heart," and one is hard put to say upon which note the final chord is constructed.

It follows that the whole question of order, which is the primary theme of the novel, is never resolved in any explicit fashion. Forster is never able—or willing—to draw precisely the line where inclusion must stop and exclusion begin, but he is

12 Reuben A. Brower, "Beyond E. M. Forster: The Unseen," *The Chicago Review*, II (Fall–Winter, 1948), 109.

at any rate sure of certain elements that must make part of his new order. Personal relations, love, form, comprehensiveness, reason, intuitive understanding: all, though perhaps limited or partial, are necessary, but Forster stops short of a final synthesis. Perhaps he himself realized the impossibility of one, for, while in *Howards End* Margaret Schlegel was meant to be the cynosure of all the ideals related to connecting, in *A Passage to India* there is a distribution among several people—Fielding, Mrs. Moore, Godbole, Aziz—of the qualities that are meant to be admired. Forster is indicating the paths that lead away from chaos, but he does not make them join; there is no Howards End to serve as the all-embracing symbol of the good life. *A Passage to India* directs the reader back to life again. It is a vision, not an answer, an echo and a counterecho whose monotonous and hopeful sounds spread back through India the primal to the world that was before man and forward through the present to a future that man must make for himself.

5 · Art and Order

AFTER A *Passage to India,* Forster published no more novels; [1] nonetheless, his concern with the problem of order continued as an integral part of his nonfictional writing, in which, curiously, the problem was at last resolved (as far as any problem could be resolved in Forster's world) by an affirmation of art. The solution seems curious because the novels attack so forcefully, if not art, then the aesthetic view of life, and because so little positive is said in them about art itself. Indeed, one generally feels that art is a force for the bad in the fiction, and, although the impression is erroneous, it is understandable, since it arises from the constant association of an *interest in* art with inactivity and sterility. The fact is that Forster makes no conscious effort in the novels to distinguish between the arts in themselves and the uses his characters make of them, but some discrminations are made, implicitly, among the uses at least, and these adumbrate Forster's later and more reasoned beliefs. On the one hand, there are figures like Philip, Rickie, and Cecil, who, in their imposition of the forms and categories of painting upon life, stand back, as from an easel, to contemplate it; on the other, there are the far less frequent characters like

1 Forster did, however, write one more novel, apparently before 1927 (see *The Letters of T. E. Lawrence,* ed. by David Garnett [New York: Doubleday, Doran & Co., Inc., 1939] p. 537, where Lawrence refers to the novel in a letter to Forster), besides a fragment, entitled *Arctic Summer,* which comes chronologically before *Howards End* (see Angus Wilson, "A Conversation with E. M. Forster," p. 55; and Furbank and Haskell, pp. 24–27).

Lucy Honeychurch, who, in her love of music, finds freedom from her cousin Charlotte's oppressively limited ideas and codes of behavior.

It is easy enough to understand why Forster should have symbolized the attitudes he disliked through an interest in painting or pictures particularly. The characteristic approaches to that art—looking, viewing, seeing, contemplating—suggest distance, detachment; pictures themselves, framed and hung, proclaim, more obviously than works of literature or music, the fact that they are isolated and apart from the confusion of ordinary reality. Music, on the contrary, suggests to Forster—probably to most people—a more flexible, a less constricting form; it seems closer to the mysteries at the heart of the universe, and, not surprisingly, it has always seemed to Forster the art that underlies all the others. Furthermore, Forster generally conceives of music as something to be shared. Its spirit encourages participation, mutual understanding, as in *Where Angels Fear to Tread*, where even Philip learns, at least in part, to transcend his characteristic passivity; or as in "Co-ordination," where Miss Haddon, listening to the sounds of a seashell, learns about the sources of Melody and Victory. In addition music fosters a different spirit in its appreciators than literature and painting do: if the counterpart of the writer is the reader, of the painter, the viewer, music alone permits a player as well as a listener, one who cooperates actively, even physically, with the composer of the music he performs. So, in *A Room with a View*, Forster writes of his heroine, "who loved to play on the side of Victory":

It so happened that Lucy, who found daily life chaotic, entered a more solid world when she opened the piano. . . . The kingdom of music is not the kingdom of this world. . . . The commonplace person begins to play, and shoots into the empyrean without effort, whilst we look up, marvelling how he has escaped us, and thinking how we could worship and love him, would he but translate his visions into human words, and his experiences into actions. Perhaps he cannot; certainly he does not, or does so very seldom. (p. 40)

Lucy does eventually translate her experiences into action, partly, it seems, because in the kingdom of music she learns to cope with chaotic daily life, not, like Philip, by seeing around it, but by entering into it. "Lucy never knew her desires so clearly as after music. . . . She wanted something big" (p. 52). At the piano, Lucy is suddenly aware of the greater possibilities of her own life, and eventually she learns to realize her intimations, for, as Mr. Beebe asks, "Does it seem reasonable that she should play so wonderfully, and live so quietly? I suspect that one day she will be wonderful in both. The water-tight compartments in her will break down, and music and life will mingle" (p. 113). Music encourages its lovers to break down artificial barriers, while painting helps its devotees to erect them: herein lies the basis of Forster's contrast.

It has already been suggested that this contrast falsifies, or at least takes no account of, Forster's feelings about works of art considered as entities in themselves. One suspects that he was too much concerned with the artistic vision that limited some of his characters' growth, too busy fighting in himself the tendencies he embodied in them to think much about the value of art. His treatment of writers and writing makes this point clearer: Miss Raby, the novelist in "The Eternal Moment," is Forster's most ambiguous study of the relation between literature and life; Rickie Elliot, Forster's closest approach to a self-portrait, is made to disparage his stories, and his descriptions of them indicate that they are the stories Forster himself wrote. To be sure, the heaven of "The Celestial Omnibus" is populated mainly with literary figures and their authors (there is music there, but no painting), but the objectionable Mr. Bons in that same story is Forster's most prominent litterateur. At any rate, it was only when he had achieved sufficient distance himself from the writing of novels and short stories, only when, paradoxically, he was no longer involved in the creation of fiction, that Forster began to look more discriminatingly at works of art and, by approving what he found, was able to complete the search for stability and permanence that is the subject of all his earlier work.

The antiaesthetic attitude is still apparent in Forster's nonfiction, but it is now directed largely against the art of criticism, while the value of creative writing is increasingly affirmed. Criti-

cism and creation come to take the roles that the detached
spectator and the active participant played in the novels. Indeed, if the Philips and Cecils of the novels are, to their detri-
ment, the critics of life, it is their type also who are, in Forster's
opinion, the critics of art. Forster does have some appreciative
remarks to make about criticism—its "central job seems to be
education through precision" (*TC*, p. 109); it helps, or should
help, to train us to look at the work and not at ourselves, and,
at best, to prepare the way for a correct approach to the deepest
experience that art has to offer. But most often Forster is, despite his own role as critic, on the offensive; indeed the uncer-
tain attitude toward himself that leads in the novels to the
harsh treatment of such characters as Rickie manifests itself in
the nonfiction in Forster's handling of critics. He suspects them
of robbing the work of its meaning by neatly categorizing it in
some convenient period or type or school. He objects, too, that
criticism rarely helps the artist and rarely meets the work of
art in the proper spirit of freshness and innocence: sophistica-
tion and judgment trip the critic up and leave him looking *at*
the artist, not *with* him. But most of all he resents the fact that
criticism "teaches us everything about the book except the central thing, and between that and us it raises a circular barrier
which only the wings of the spirit can cross" (*TC*, p. 85).
Criticism cannot, any more than the aesthetic characters in the
stories, penetrate to the poetry at the heart of things that is so
readily accessible to the more primitive figures. It is always, like
Fielding in *A Passage to India*, missing something it feels to be
there because of its inevitably limited approach.

To the limitations of criticism Forster opposes the more
relaxed and personal expansiveness of the creative state. Criticism "has to withdraw when reality approaches" (*TC*, p. 117);
it is conscious, intellectual, rational, knows what it is doing before it does it; as such, it is, for Forster, concerned with the
surface, with what is external, rather than with the central mystery that he finds in creativity, as in all forms of communication. He writes:

[In the creative state] a man is taken out of himself. He lets down
as it were a bucket into his subconsciousness, and draws up something which is normally beyond his reach. He mixes this thing with

his normal experiences, and out of the mixture he makes a work of art. . . . Whether it is good or bad it will have been compounded in this unusual way, and he will wonder afterwards how he did it. (*TC*, p. 114)

This idea recurs in Forster's work. In *Aspects of the Novel*, he imagines a group of writers from different centuries sitting around a table and all experiencing much the same thing, having "entered a common state which it is convenient to call inspiration" (p. 23). In "Anonymity," the essay in which the central statement of his belief in this "common state" appears, Forster stresses the fact that all minds have two personalities, the "upper" and the "lower." The lower, into which the artist must dip his bucket, "has something in common with all other deeper personalities" (*TC*, p. 84). Indeed, in the fiction, it is at this deeper level that one finds the meaning of great moments and of the ineffable quality of the redemptive characters; here are located the inexplicable influences that inspire or compel Mrs. Wilcox and Mrs. Moore, that Lucy feels when she plays piano, that are present at the Hindu festival or at Adela's trial, that encourage and sustain the friendship of Mrs. Moore and Aziz. And it is to this level that one must come—to a state like the artist's in the creative act—if one is to appreciate a work of art properly. "What is so wonderful about great literature," Forster writes, "is that it transforms the man who reads it towards the condition of the man who wrote, and brings to birth in us also the creative impulse" (*Ibid.*). Works of art tend toward a state of anonymity; they want to be unsigned, to call attention to themselves and not to their authors, for they are the product of this deeper, prelogical state common to all men. The critic is ultimately ineffective, not only because he usually fails at what is his legitimate task, but because he is generally unwilling or unable, given his ordinary approach, to lower his own bucket into what William James similarly called the deep well of the unconscious.

Whether Forster's account of the creative experience is accurate is obviously impossible to determine, and probably irrelevant—most artists have their own accounts—but it does explain a good deal about his attitudes. One can understand, in the first place, why Forster looks with misgiving upon attempts to portray him as a highly conscious artist: he has always insisted that in his writing a good deal more "happens" than he foresees or deliberately plans. It indicates, too, why he dislikes the idea of tracing an author's development, an idea implying a more logical scheme in the sequence of the writer's work, perhaps even a more conscious striving in that writer, than Forster is willing to admit. In spite of his strictures, however, one is tempted to think of Forster himself as a careful and patient artist, aware of those symbols and rhythms in his novels which seem to indicate so much forethought and planning.[2] But whatever Forster's method of work, it is easy to detect the rationale of his attitude toward it: the critic is easily identified as the outsider, the spectator, the man cut off from life or art in its most vital forms; the creative writer, on the other hand, is able to participate and to communicate successfully. These equations do not express new values; they simply introduce new terms.

Forster's own criticism, it must be said, does attempt to fulfill his concept of the critic's job: to consider always the created object itself rather than the period or even the author; to lead the reader as close as possible to what is ultimately inexplicable, to encourage, clarify, appreciate, but then to leave him to make his own contact with the work of art. Admitting and accepting the creative act, without attempting, in any ultimate sense, to understand or to analyze it, Forster, as critic, accepts a modest role as servant of the creator. Apart from "Anonymity" (and, of course, *Aspects of the Novel*, in which a constant watch is kept on the tendency to dogmatize, and in which the discussion centers mainly on the particular components of art rather than on the more abstract concept of art in general), Forster's most important theoretical essays fall within a relatively short period of time. In fact, although he appears to have formulated his basic ideas about art early in his career, he developed and wrote about them at length almost exclusively during and shortly after the Second World War, in the decade between 1939 and 1949. Before the outbreak of war, Forster had in his essays only sporadically noted the quali-

2 Forster does not, of course, explicitly deny the conscious element in art, but his stress, throughout his criticism, lies elsewhere.

ties he felt to be important in works of art. In *Aspects of the Novel*, for example, after a discussion of the difficulties of communication, he writes:

But in the novel we can know people perfectly, and, apart from the general pleasure of reading, we can find here a compensation for their dimness in life. In this direction fiction is truer than history, because it goes beyond the evidence, and each of us knows from his own experience that there is something beyond the evidence. . . . And that is why novels, even when they are about wicked people, can solace us; they suggest a more comprehensible and thus a more manageable human race, they give us the illusion of perspicacity and of power. (p. 62)

All of us, Forster says, yearn for permanence, and permanence is what a work of art suggests by creating what is in fact a new world, a world in which people and their motives are understandable and in which the baffling and disturbing lacunae of real life can be explained. This idea Forster later developed fully, but even at this point one sees the beginnings of a theory that will make of each artistic work a unique and organic whole, an order that, in its internal coherence, is totally unlike the chaos of day-to-day living.

After the war had begun, Forster attributed the power of art to its association with tradition and to its ability to join work and pleasure. These reasons, along with those given in the quotation from *Aspects of the Novel*, suggest a central meaning for the several values that art came to have for Forster. As an ideal, it grew to represent in the nonfiction what in the fiction was symbolized, variously and with some hesitance, by the continuity of English country life, by the spirit of the generations, by the more "natural" life of the Italians, by the connecting of the disparate elements of twentieth-century life, even by personal relations. Art became the chief answer to life's daily gray, to the limitations of communication, to the restlessness and flux of modern urban living. Perhaps the disillusionment that is apparent in *A Passage to India* involved a final loss of confidence in the values that, however tentatively held, had been implicit and explicit in the previous novels and therefore made the search for a new direction imperative. To be sure, there is much praise of the past in the nonfiction, but with it comes

the awareness that it cannot be taken over whole and unchanged into the present; there is in the nonfiction, too, a definite affirmation of personal relations, but it is accompanied by
the knowledge that understanding is always imperfect and that
relationships are inevitably subject to the condition of change.
The ideal of art is independent of time, of place, of people,
and to it in the end Forster turned, discerning there something
unique, the power to make humanity more comprehensible and
manageable, and he gave form to his discovery in his variant of
the theory of art for art's sake.[3]

Forster nowhere seeks consciously to substitute art for life;
indeed he disclaims any connection with the self-conscious
aestheticism of critics like Oscar Wilde. "Many things, besides
art, matter" (TC, p. 89), he writes, and indeed many other
things do matter to Forster: his hostility to the confusion of art
with life is apparent in the novels, and even in the nonfiction
his claims for art are qualified. But what he does claim for it
is a great deal:

[The phrase "art for art's sake"] is a profound phrase. It indicates
that art is a self-contained harmony. Art is valuable not because it
is educational (though it may be), not because it is recreative
(though it may be), not because everyone enjoys it (for everybody
does not), not even because it has to do with beauty. It is valuable
because it has to do with order, and creates little worlds of its own,
possessing internal harmony, in the bosom of this disordered planet.
It is needed at once and now. It is needed before it is appreciated
and independent of appreciation. . . . It is the activity which
brought man out of original darkness and differentiates him from
the beasts, and we must continue to practise and respect it through
the darkness of today. (TC, pp. 59–60)

This statement makes a good deal clear. One sees, first of all,
why art gives a feeling of permanence—it is a self-contained
harmony; one sees why it can solace us—it presents worlds that
are unlike our own disordered universe; one sees why Forster
connects it with tradition and why he stresses it in time of war
—it is the record of man's greatest needs and greatest accomplishments.

Furthermore, art is the *only* area in which Forster finds

3 See Professor Johnstone's The Bloomsbury Group, Chapter III.

order. "Viewed realistically," he comments, "the past is really a series of *dis*orders succeeding one another by discoverable laws, no doubt, and certainly marked by an increasing growth of human interference, but disorders all the same" (*TC,* p. 90). Works of art are "little vantage grounds in the changing chaos" (*TC,* p. 94), and it is these vantage grounds that Forster has always sought. In them he found at last a safe passage between the Scylla and Charybdis of a too stringent and debilitating order on the one side and absolute confusion on the other. In one sense, as has been suggested, Forster acknowledged the failure of many of his old hopes in this affirmation of art, hopes that had been projected and tested in his five novels and one by one abandoned; but in another sense he managed to leave at least one door open for them in his new house of art. Art is, for Forster, in the widest sense, moral; although—or perhaps because—it is self-contained, it conveys certain truths to all men. In the pertinacity of art, Forster writes, he sees increasingly "something more and more profound, something which does in fact concern people who do not care about art at all" (*Ibid.*). This "something" represents the constant summons to man to strive for order in his own sphere, to fight, even with the foreknowledge of failure, against the iron laws of flux and change.

The theory of art for art's sake, then, provided Forster with a solution of sorts, but one that proved to be, as well, itself a stimulus to new questions. "By the side of the everlasting Why," Mr. Emerson tells Lucy Honeychurch, "there is a Yes— a transitory Yes if you like, but a Yes" (p. 38). In his non-fiction Forster won through to his Yes—a transitory Yes, and he has continued to affirm, if with somewhat less resilience and vigor, his old beliefs. More important, however, is the paradoxical fact that, implicitly, Forster had much earlier both testified to his faith in art as order and put that belief into practice: prior to theory, his novels and stories represent the successful achievement of order in art. Though art is not discussed as a positive force in the novels in any important way, though the novels embody a struggle against the aesthetic view of life, still they are, as entities, what the essays preach: they are Forster's illustration of that order about which he began to speak only after he had himself ceased to produce fiction. They are, whatever their subjects or moods or tones, assertions of the possibility of order in one area certainly and, hopefully, in others as well. They *are* orders, however bleak the vision of life some of them present, and so they stand as the validation of the theory that was born only after the impulse to produce them had died.

In cases where the first edition of one of Forster's works has not been used, the date of original publication is given in parentheses. The Uniform Pocket Edition of Forster's works, published by Edward Arnold & Co., is not yet complete; those volumes that have already appeared in this series are used, and, for the others, editions readily available to an American reader are listed.

I. WORKS BY FORSTER

Books

Abinger Harvest. London: Edward Arnold & Co., 1953 (1936).

Alexandria, A History and A Guide. 2nd ed. Alexandria: Whitehead Morris Ltd., 1938 (1922).

Aspects of the Novel. London: Edward Arnold & Co., 1953 (1927).

The Collected Tales of E. M. Forster. New York: Alfred A. Knopf, 1952 (*The Celestial Omnibus and Other Stories*, 1911; *The Eternal Moment and Other Stories*, 1928).

England's Pleasant Land: A Pageant Play. London: The Hogarth Press, 1940.

Goldsworthy Lowes Dickinson. London: Edward Arnold & Co., 1947 (1934).

The Hill of Devi. New York: Harcourt, Brace & Co., 1953.

Howards End. London: Edward Arnold & Co., 1951 (1910).

The Longest Journey. London: Edward Arnold & Co., 1947
  (1907).
Marianne Thorton: A Domestic Biography, 1797–1887. New
  York: Harcourt, Brace & Co., 1956.
A Passage to India. London: Edward Arnold & Co., 1953
  (1924).
Pharos and Pharillon. 3rd ed. London: The Hogarth Press,
  1926 (1923).
A Room with a View. London: Edward Arnold & Co., 1952
  (1908).
Two Cheers for Democracy. New York: Harcourt, Brace & Co.,
  1951.
Where Angels Fear to Tread. London: Edward Arnold & Co.,
  1953 (1905).

Uncollected Material: A Selection

"Albergo Empedocle," *Temple Bar,* CXXVIII (December,
  1903), 663–84.
"The Blue Boy," *The Listener,* LVII (March 14, 1957), 444.
"Dante," *The Working Men's College Journal,* X (February,
  1908), 261–64; X (March, 1908), 281–86; X (April, 1908),
  301–6.
"De Senectute," *The London Magazine,* IV (November, 1957),
  15–18.
"Erotic Indian Sculpture," *The Listener,* LXI (March 12,
  1959), 469–71.
"Fog Over Ferney," *The Listener,* LX (December 18, 1958),
  1029–30.
"A Great Humanist," *The Listener,* LVI (October 11, 1956),
  545–47.
"Indian Entries," *Encounter,* XVIII (January, 1962), 20–27.
"Introduction," *The Warm Country,* by Donald Windham.
  New York: Charles Scribner's Sons, n.d.
"A Letter," *The Twentieth Century,* XLVII (February, 1955),
  99–101.
"Letters" in *Letters to T. E. Lawrence.* Edited by A. W. Law-
  rence. London: Jonathan Cape, 1962.

"Nordic Twilight," *England Speaks: A Symposium*. New York: The Macmillan Co., 1941 (1940), pp. 55–83.

"Notes," *A Passage to India*. ("Everyman's Library.") London: J. M. Dent & Sons Ltd., 1942.

"Pessimism in Literature," *The Working Men's College Journal*, X (January, 1907), 6–10; X (February, 1907), 26–33.

"Recollections of Nassenheide," *The Listener*, LXI (January 1, 1959), 12–14.

"Tourism v. Thuggism," *The Listener*, LVII (January 17, 1957), 124.

"A View Without a Room," *The Observer*, No. 8717 (July 27, 1958), 15

II. WORKS ON FORSTER

Books

Beer, J. B. *The Achievement of E. M. Forster*. New York: Barnes & Noble, 1962.

Brown, E. K. *Rhythm in the Novel*. Toronto: University of Toronto Press, 1950.

Crews, Frederick C. *E. M. Forster: The Perils of Humanism*. Princeton, N. J.: Princeton University Press, 1962.

Grandsen, K. W. *E. M. Forster*. New York: Grove Press, 1962.

Johnstone, J. K. *The Bloomsbury Group: A Study of E. M. Forster, Lytton Strachey, Virginia Woolf, and Their Circle*. New York: The Noonday Press, 1954.

Macaulay, Rose. *The Writings of E. M. Forster*. London: The Hogarth Press, 1938.

McConkey, James. *The Novels of E. M. Forster*. Ithaca, N. Y.: Cornell University, 1957.

Oliver, H. J. *The Art of E. M. Forster*. London: Melbourne University Press, 1960.

Trilling, Lionel. *E. M. Forster*. Norfolk, Conn.: New Directions Books, 1943.

Warner, Rex. *E. M. Forster*. London: Published for the British Council and the National Book League by Longmans, Green & Co., 1950.

Articles: A Selection

Ault, Peter. "Aspects of E. M. Forster," *The Dublin Review*, CCXIX (October, 1946), 109–34.

Belgion, Montgomery. "The Diabolism of Mr. E. M. Forster," *The Criterion*, XIV (October, 1934), 54–73.

Brower, Reuben A. "Beyond E. M. Forster: Part I—The Earth," *Foreground*, I (Spring–Summer, 1946), 164–74.

——. "Beyond E. M. Forster: The Unseen," *The Chicago Review*, II (Fall–Winter, 1948), 102–12.

——. *The Fields of Light: An Experiment in Critical Reading.* New York: Oxford University Press, 1951.

Burra, Peter. "Introduction," to E. M. Forster's *A Passage to India.* ("Everyman's Library.") London: J. M. Dent & Sons Ltd., 1942.

Cecil, Lord David. *Poets and Story-Tellers.* New York: The Macmillan Co., 1949.

Connolly, Cyril. *Enemies of Promise.* Revised ed. New York: The Macmillan Co., 1948, pp. 26–27 and *passim.*

Cox, C. B. *The Free Spirit.* London: Oxford University Press, 1963.

Dobrée, Bonamy. *The Lamp and the Lute: Studies in Six Modern Authors.* Oxford: Oxford University Press, 1929.

Furbank, P. N., and Haskell, F. J. H. "E. M. Forster," *Writers at Work.* Edited by Malcolm Cowley. New York: The Viking Press, 1958.

Fussell, Paul, Jr. "E. M. Forster's Mrs. Moore: Some Suggestions," *Philological Quarterly*, XXXII (October, 1953), 388–95.

Gerber, Helmut E. "E. M. Forster: An Annotated Checklist of Writings About Him," *English Fiction in Transition*, II (Spring, 1959), 4–27.

Hall, James. *The Tragic Comedians.* Bloomington, Ind.: Indiana University Press, 1963.

Harvey, John. "Imagination and Moral Theme in E. M. Forster's *The Longest Journey*," *Essays in Criticism*, VI (October, 1956), 418–33.

Hoare, Dorothy M. *Some Studies in the Modern Novel.* London: Chatto & Windus, 1938.

Holt, Lee Elbert. "E. M. Forster and Samuel Butler," *PMLA*, LXI (September, 1946), 804–19.

Jones, David. "E. M. Forster on his Life and his Books," *The Listener*, LXI (January 1, 1959), 11–12.

Kermode, Frank. *Puzzles and Epiphanies*. London: Routledge & Kegan Paul, 1962.

Leavis, F. R. "E. M. Forster," *Scrutiny*, VII (September, 1938), 185–202.

———. "Meet Mr. Forster," *Scrutiny*, XII (Autumn, 1944), 308–9.

McDowell, Frederick P. W. " 'The Mild, Intellectual Light': Idea and Theme in *Howards End*," *PMLA*, LXXIV (September, 1959), 453–63.

Modern Fiction Studies. E. M. Forster Number. VII (Autumn, 1961).

Richards, I. A. "A Passage to Forster: Reflections on a Novelist," *Forum*, LXXVIII (December, 1927), 914–20.

Savage, D. S. *The Withered Branch: Six Studies in the Modern Novel*. London: Eyre & Spottiswoode, 1950.

Shusterman, David. "The Curious Case of Professor Godbole: *A Passage to India* Re-examined," *PMLA*, LXXVI (September, 1961) 426–35.

Spender, Stephen. *The Creative Element*. London: Hamish Hamilton, 1953.

Warren, Austin. *Rage for Order*. Chicago: University of Chicago Press, 1948.

Wilson, Angus. "A Conversation with E. M. Forster," *Encounter*, IX (November, 1957), 52–57.

———. "The Revolt of Samuel Butler," *The Atlantic Monthly*, CC (November, 1957), 190–98.

Woolf, Virginia. *The Death of the Moth and Other Essays*. London: The Hogarth Press, 1942.

Zabel, Morton Dauwen. *Craft and Character; Texts, Method, and Vocation in Modern Fiction*. New York: The Viking Press, 1957.